Breathtaking

A PERSONAL TESTIMONY BY
AMBER NICOLE METZ

Breathtaking

Pleasant Word
A Division of WINEPRESS PUBLISHING

Pleasant Word (a division of WinePress Publishing, PO Box 428, Enumclaw, WA 98022) functions only as book publisher. As such, the ultimate design, content, editorial accuracy, and views expressed or implied in this work are those of the author.

Unless otherwise noted, all Scriptures are taken from the New American Standard Bible, © 1960, 1963, 1968, 1971, 1972, 1973, 1975, 1977 by The Lockman Foundation. Used by permission.

Scripture references marked NIV are taken from the *Holy Bible, New International Version®, NIV®*. Copyright © 1973, 1978, 1984 by the International Bible Society. Used by permission of Zondervan. All rights reserved.

Scripture references marked KJV are taken from the King James Version of the Bible.

Scripture references marked AMP are taken from The Amplified Bible, Old Testament, © 1965 and 1987 by The Zondervan Corporation, and from The Amplified New Testament, © 1954, 1958, 1987 by The Lockman Foundation. Used by permission.

ISBN 13: 978-1-4141-0897-1
ISBN 10: 1-4141-0897-4
Library of Congress Catalog Card Number: 2006910113

Dedication

Jesus,
Make me the breath of God. Thank You for loving me for the
dreamer I am and mending my broken heart time and time
again. I want You...for You alone are Worthy.

The unnamed Saints in Hebrews 11:35-40:
You are my inspiration.

From June 26, 2005…

I want to dream, to listen and, most of all, to obey and go wherever He leads. It's true; most people never truly listen. But I want to hear the whispers, see the faint rustle of the trees, and allow my heart and mind to go places they've never gone before. I'm tired of the typical, the predictable, and the safe. I want more. I won't settle for anything less than God's best, and you better believe I'm going to have to continue to lay down everything I've already been given, continuing to walk by faith and not by sight, in order to receive my orders from my King.

Amber Nicole Metz

Table of Contents

Preface

BUCK & KRISTIN SUTTON

"Let no one look down on your youthfulness, but rather in speech, conduct, love, faith and purity, show yourself an example of those who believe."

—1 Timothy 4:12

Amber Nicole Metz may be only in her twenties, but this young woman has a nonnegotiable passion for absolute truth that does not take long to notice once you meet her. Things have not always been this way, though.

Although we have known Amber since she was a baby, it was not until the year 2000 that we began to have close contact with her through our ministry, *Teens for Christ*, where our vision statement is, "To turn teenagers into fully committed followers of Jesus Christ." A chapter opened up in her school district the second semester of her freshman year of high school, and we asked her to lead the charge on getting people there to hear the gospel. Amber attended those meetings and began to grow immensely in her faith. At the end of her sophomore year of high school, she felt called to be a part of our TFC ministry team, which travels to churches around the area to minister to them in song and skit. Each year the team consists of teenagers who are serious about their faith and want higher accountability and growth in their spiritual walk.

As Amber became involved on the team, it was apparent her health was declining. She would have severe coughing episodes that would last for minutes, take her breath away, and cause her face to turn blue, but she never told anyone about her cystic fibrosis or acknowledged that it was a problem. Even when she stood before congregations, she never mentioned the severity of her illness. She was clearly in denial. Our leadership team would pull her aside and discuss her illness, encouraging her to be open and real with the body of Christ, but we also realized that would not be possible without Amber herself coming to terms with the fact that she had a terminal illness.

After spending two years on the ministry team and slowly beginning to come to terms with her physical condition, Amber set off for Cedarville University, where God began to work on her even more and take her on a journey that would brand her heart. As she fought for survival, she not only came to terms with the reality of her illness but also realized that God in His sovereignty had an amazing plan for her life. While she was gravely ill, through writing emails to hundreds across the nation, she had the opportunity to glorify Him in ways most of us may never have the privilege of doing. Now those emails have been turned into this book—*Breathtaking*. Amber gives all the glory back to her heavenly Father and is consumed with a passion to see the American church flourish and to be an instrument God uses to evangelize the world and make disciples in His name.

Now, over two years since surgery, Amber is full of vigor and vitality. She realizes, though, that even after receiving a double lung transplant, her life will probably still be much shorter than her peers'. In Amber's mind, this is far from unfair. Instead it is the avenue God has given her to bring glory to Himself. This young woman will allow nothing to hinder her calling or bridle her passion for Christ. She desires that this same level of intensity will be a lifestyle for the ones closest to her. She is relentless in her message and disgusted with status-quo Christianity, longing for others to feel the same passion she feels.

As you read *Breathtaking*, we pray you will sense Amber's heart for her Savior and Lord as well as her desire to see others experience our God for who He is. Amber has dedicated her life to seeing others ignited with the fire of the truth that fuels every breath she takes. We don't know where *Breathtaking* will take her, but we celebrate her obedience to His calling and praise Him for the opportunity to know and minister alongside her.

Buck & Kristin Sutton
www.teens-for-christ.com
December 2007

Acknowledgements

Father, Son & Holy Spirit: *Oh, Father, how can I ever express my love for You? Empty me, Jesus, and fill me with You and Your Word. Burn within me a passion for only You. While I am still alive, use me—please Father—just use me for Your fame and Your renown (Isaiah 26:8). May others see You in me and be drawn toward your love, toward the only One who can set them free. Thank You for letting me fly. I am amazed.*

MY FAMILY:

Daddy, Mom & Holly:

Thank you for believing in my crazy dreams and loving me when I am so unlovable; you have truly seen me at my worst. I love you all more than words can ever convey, and I pray that I will honor you as I continue on my journey.

Grandpa & Grandma Jump:

Thank you for all the memories of the past, for the present and the future, for all the after-school meals when I was little, but especially for all the reams of paper and countless cartridges of ink I used in the past year. I love you.

Grandpa & Grandma Metz:

I miss and love you both dearly. Even though I wish you could be here with me now, I am so thankful you are Home with Jesus. I hope I make you proud.

Everyone else:

I love you all and am so thankful to be able to call each of you a member of my family.

My Friends:

To those of you who are represented in *Breathtaking* and those of you who are not, you are my greatest earthly treasures and "I love you" is the understatement of the century. They say if one goes through life with one best friend, they are blessed; if that's the case, I broke the bank with all of you. Thank you all for making me a better person and for allowing me into your lives, even if only for a season. I love you all and would die for any of you in a split second. We made it, guys.

Teens for Christ, Lima, Ohio:

Buck & Kristin and the rest of the staff, here and abroad:

I am honored to be so closely connected with such a powerful ministry. You all have taken me in and taught me much more than I will ever be able to thank you for. For all the staff meetings you've let me sit in on, the paper and ink I've used, for the times you let me say what I really thought about things (OK, so I usually do that anyway), and for letting me cry in one of your respective offices— it all means so much. Thank you for coming alongside me and showing me there is a better way, for making me face my fears and fall facedown before my Savior. Oh, and Annie, I love you and our Wednesdays out of the office together!

Never stop dreaming, guys. No matter where the Lord takes me, you will always go with me...even if I'm speaking in yet another field full of twenty people!

Lima Baptist Temple & other surrounding churches:

Thank you for allowing me to come and minister to your congregations in the past year, even if all I had was myself, my Bible, and my God-given passion. You accepted me with open arms and allowed me to pour out my heart. Thank you for the kind words of encouragement and helpful suggestions and constructive criticisms that have made me a better disciple of Jesus and a clearer presenter of His Truth.

Anonymous financial donors to the publication of *Breathtaking*:

This book would not be possible without each and every one of you. Whether you gave a few dollars or thousands, your donation will make an impact on the Kingdom and I can never say "thank you" enough. I honor you and your financial contribution to *Breathtaking* and Breathtaking Ministries. No matter where I go, it is those who believed in the project from the beginning whom I will never forget.

Toledo Children's Hospital & Columbus Children's Hospital:

Dr. Vauthy and Mary, Shawn Teller and Mandy O'Brien, Dr. Astor, Karen, Julie, Polly, Jen Russel and everyone else: thank you from the bottom of my heart for taking care of me and making me feel wonderfully loved and cherished.

Cedarville University and Moody Bible Institute:

Dr. Brown, Pastor Rohm & the rest of the CU Family:

I spent only four short months with you, but I feel you will be a part of me forever. Cedarville was where I learned how to fly in His arms. The opportunities He afforded me while I was there were the catalyst for *Breathtaking*. I love you all, and

I cannot wait to see what God has in store for the campus and for all of you.

Moody Bible Institute:

Thank you for not kicking me out in the winter of 2005 when I dropped out of my online classes due to feeling as though I was too weak to finish the class work I started after leaving CU. I also distinctly remember telling the school that "the Lord was calling me to focus only on studying His Word, reading other books, and writing emails to people about my life and, whether the administration understood or not, I was dropping out of my courses until further notice." I think that was the wording I used to one of the administrators in February of 2005. In any case, I am back and actually doing my work now, thankful that Moody didn't think I was crazy and has fully supported me every step of the way. I love you all and look forward to finishing my Biblical Studies degree. Thank you for allowing me to be obedient to His calling, even when I didn't understand what I was doing!

Authors, Pastors and Theologians:

Thank you to the following: D.A. Carson, Mark Buchanan, Mark Driscoll, Louie Giglio, Jeremy Kimble, Kyle Lake, C.S. Lewis, James MacDonald, Erwin McManus, Beth Moore, Andrew Murray, George Muller, Dr. John Piper, James & Betty Robison, Andy Stanley, A.W. Tozer, Matthew Paul Turner, Dan Wigton, Dallas Willard, Philip Yancey, and many others whom I have yet to discover—those who have made me think "outside of the box" and ultimately take a stand for what I know is true: the holistic gospel and the anticipation of the full redemption one day, when we no longer see in part but in whole and finally see our Lord face-to-face (1 Corinthians 13:12). Thank you for sharing in His sufferings and being such usable vessels for His glory.

Winepress & Pleasant Word, esp. Athena Dean, Tim Noreen & Adam Cothes:

Thank you for believing in my passion, for helping me see it come into fruition, and for standing beside me every step of the way. I feel privileged to write for your company but, more importantly, to have the honor of serving my Savior through this powerful vehicle.

You, the reader:

May you come to know the living God through reading *Breathtaking.* As you walk with me—as I remember my journey—please do not think highly of me but instead of Jesus Christ, the One who set me free. I love you all.

Breathtaking

"The man who writes about himself in his own time, is the only man who writes about all people and about all time."
—George Bernard Shaw

*B*reathtaking was not born out of earthly joy but out of heavenly brokenness—a brokenness before my heavenly Father and countless other individuals. One day God spoke to me more clearly than He ever had before. He took me through a valley that cut me to the core, showing me that I am not Superwoman (contrary to what I had believed for years) and that no matter how hard I try, I can do nothing without Him.

After battling cystic fibrosis since birth, I was told at the age of nineteen to leave the college I adored to come home to wait for a double lung transplant. I was never guaranteed the transplant would come in time or that it would be successful.

But Jesus did promise me one thing: He would go before me and bring to fruition everything in my life He had established since before the foundations of time. What that meant exactly was none of my concern. I was never promised to see my twentieth birthday, marriage, or children. I was to follow the road less traveled and leave behind everything on this earth that I clung to for security, take up my cross, and follow hard after Him into the unknown (Matthew 16:24-25).

In return, the Lord met me in my weakness and taught me that His strength is indeed made strong in my weakness (2 Corinthians 12:9). Once I let go of my selfish pride, I finally felt the freedom that comes in His name (Isaiah 61:1-3) and I set out on a mission to make my life a living sacrifice (Romans 12:1) for the kingdom of God. Although I did not understand His ways, I wanted to be obedient to His will—no matter whether that meant I lived or died.

During the whole ordeal, I longed not to be trapped in an earthly vessel that hated me and with a soul that believed Satan's lies. My spirit was so willing, yet my flesh was so weak. I could barely breathe, but from March to Christmas Day of 2005 I poured my heart out through more than 165 emails to countless individuals. This book is composed of some of those gut-wrenching accounts of how I felt physically, emotionally, and spiritually during those long, soul-stirring months—like a modern day *A Grief Observed* by C.S. Lewis. There are also reflections from several people who were close to the situation in order to give a broader perspective on the journey. From planning my funeral, to experiencing two false alarms before my double lung transplant, to finding beauty in the simplicity of every breath, it's all here. It is my love offering to my Savior and my privilege to share it with His creation.

Just over a year since my life-giving surgery, I am at a loss for words as to how to introduce what the Lord allowed me to go through and subsequently share with readers. For months I have contemplated what I would say, even writing out rough drafts. In the end, since everything I penned did not seem to flow, I sit here doing what I was created to do: pour my heart out to my Savior and His people and leave the rest to His Holy Spirit.

You see, I do not find almost dying at the age of nineteen a curse from Satan, but instead, a divine privilege and opportunity from Jesus Christ. I can proclaim two things: He is sovereign and He is good—no matter what happens. At times, I did not know if I would survive physically and/or emotionally, but through it all I wanted more of Him. My heart was in chains, bound by my own selfish desires and the effects of living in this fallen world. Two years earlier Jesus Christ met me in a very real and personal way by a lake at Cedarville University, and I have forever been changed.

I had no idea where this journey would (and will continue) to take me, but since I left college and came home I have never been so sure of His love for me. God didn't abandon me when He allowed me to become deathly ill; He met me and made me see the world through a different prism.

My heart's cry is to love Him for who He is instead of treating Him like a twenty-four-hour vending machine that is there to satisfy my every longing. Instead, I bask in the beauty that comes from brokenness, from being honest with the One who knows me better than I know myself. I hold fast to His sovereignty (Isaiah 55: 8-11) and count all things as loss compared to knowing Christ Jesus as more than just a history figure—but instead, my Savior and coming King (Phil. 3:8-14).

He is my oxygen, the One who gave the ultimate sacrifice for my freedom. No one has to walk through the valley of the shadow of death to feel the way I do, though. Jesus is waiting for all of us to retire our superhero capes and run into His arms, baggage and all. I am neither perfect nor have I 'arrived', but I pray that in the pages of *Breathtaking* readers discover that I am very much human—just a girl from the cornfields of northwest

Ohio. I have dreams; I have doubts and silly fears. I'm the life of the party but one of the deepest thinkers in the room at the same time. I get into fights with my parents and I have to apologize. I have thought I was in love. I love my friends and tell them more than they sometimes want to hear. I laugh hard and cry harder. I crave solitude yet long to be held and understood by other fallen human beings. More importantly, I am absolutely enamored with Jesus Christ and have pledged my allegiance solely to Him—no matter who or what I have to leave behind.

I could say so much more but I am learning that there is beauty in simplicity, in allowing the story to tell itself throughout the pages of *Breathtaking*, in swallowing my pride and falling facedown before my Savior at the end of the day in humility. I am casting all my cares on Him (1 Peter 5:6-7). The fact is, Jesus doesn't need me and the bookstores do not need another book. I also know that for His divine purposes, I am alive and publishing *Breathtaking* for such a time as this.

My joy is not found in my circumstances, in my family and friends (though I love them more than words can say), or in how many people choose to read *Breathtaking* after this sentence. He is my joy and the only constant in my life (Hebrews 13:8). I would rather die than remain silent about the work He has done in and through me and, I believe, longs to do in others, as well.

James reminds us that our lives are just a vapor that appears for a little while and then vanishes away (James 4:14). My breath was literally taken away and restored a hundredfold, but that is not what is breathtaking to me—it is having the opportunity to know Him more and trust in His Word. To me that is the essence of the word breathtaking. I could die tomorrow; who am I to say otherwise? While I am alive, though, I will embrace the One who can set me free. He's waiting.

Father, may I never forget.
Amber Nicole Metz
October 30, 2006

CHAPTER TWO

Trust

"God's love is his doing whatever needs to be done, at whatever cost, so that we will see and be satisfied with the glory of God in Jesus Christ.

Let me say it again. The love of God is his doing whatever needs to be done, at whatever cost to himself or to us, so that we will see and be satisfied by the love of God in Christ forever and ever."

—Dr. John Piper[1]

Reflections

Kent & Mary Ann Metz–Amber's parents

Our eldest daughter, Amber, was born on January 2, 1986, and weighed nine pounds and four ounces. Immediately as we watched, our newborn rapidly lost weight and lung function for no apparent reason. All we knew was that we had to get help for her, but being first-time parents, we weren't sure where to begin. We believed that God is sovereign and in control of every matter of our lives, but we could not help but be overwhelmed by the circumstances that surrounded our fragile newborn.

In March of 1986, we finally were given an answer as to why our daughter not only wasn't getting any better but was getting worse by the day. At two months of age, our beautiful baby was diagnosed with cystic fibrosis (CF)—a genetic disorder that affects the sweat glands, lungs, digestive system, and other systems within the body. After preliminary testing at our local hospital, Amber was taken to the Northwest Ohio Cystic Fibrosis Center at the Toledo Children's Hospital in Toledo, Ohio. It was there that we met Dr. Pierre Vauthy, a CF specialist who is respected worldwide. He confirmed Amber's diagnosis and admitted her into the hospital for thirty-four days, five of those being spent in the ICU. Once Amber was stabilized, we were able to take her home and resume life as normal. After being hospitalized once more for pneumonia at one-and-a-half years of age, we watched the Lord allow her to stay out of the hospital for eight more years.

At an early age, Amber's personality became apparent: she was not going to be defined by her disease. As a toddler, Amber

26

was not one who needed to be entertained; in fact, as a family we didn't have to spend much on entertainment—our daughter's antics kept us well entertained.

Thankfully, after the initial scares of her first year of life, Amber's childhood was much like that of any vibrant little girl. She always loved going to school and became involved in numerous activities, especially anything involving music. She dreamed of being a princess, had imaginary friends, and loved being with people. She loved Jesus, too, and little did we anticipate the journey He would take her on.

As the years wore on, cystic fibrosis began to take its toll on her body. Middle school was a time of adjustment. Awkward social circumstances arose, as they usually do at that age, but Amber's health was declining as well. Christmas and summer breaks from school meant one thing: a two-week period of IV antibiotics to try to combat the infection in her lungs. At times, Amber was allowed to do these treatments from home and, not to our surprise, she insisted that she complete it all without any help from us. Cystic fibrosis was not a limitation for her; it was a catalyst that only made her work harder.

Amber's high school career was filled with joys and sorrows for our family. The "clean outs" (the term used for her hospital stays) were still twice a year. Amber's total lung capacity was down to seventy-two percent the August before she started high school. By the time she entered her sophomore year it was at sixty percent. After participating in her high school's rendition of *Titanic: The Musical* in the early spring of 2002, Amber's health took a dramatic turn for the worse.

In a short four-month span, Amber's FEV1[2] went from sixty-five percent to thirty-one percent. Previously we had been able to see improvement in her lung function after intense drug therapy, but even after spending several weeks in the hospital after finishing the musical, her FEV1 rose to only thirty-five percent. (Transplants are recommended at forty percent.) At the age of sixteen Amber was faced with talks of her needing a double lung transplant sooner rather than later.

Despite all this, Amber didn't slow down. From taking a full course load, to being an active member of several clubs in her high school and attending *Teens for Christ* meetings, Amber seemed to bury herself in her work and not let her crippling disease steal her joy. Amber's love for the Lord also intensified, and the time she spent on the *Teens for Christ* ministry team only added fuel to her spiritual fire. But it was a fire that was constantly being quenched by something every time it started to grow. Pride and the inability to come to terms with her failing condition overcame her. Denial set in. Satan was feeding Amber the lie that to be weak is to be wrong. The fear that was born out of that gripped her tighter as time went on.

Her junior and senior years of high school were filled with visits to The Cleveland Clinic, where she was evaluated time and time again for a transplant. Because of Amber's determination (and stubbornness), she went to these visits with the mentality of doing everything in her power not to get listed. In her mind, transplant was not an option. She had huge dreams and had no intention of giving up on them. As parents we knew, though, that Amber's will, no matter how strong it was, wasn't going to cure her. With each passing visit, our driven daughter became more and more opposed to receiving her transplant— which in her mind was years away. We, too, had reservations about her being treated in Cleveland, but, according to our insurance, that was our only option. After more than ten visits to the center, Amber was still not listed and we began praying for other doors to open up, and even visited another center in North Carolina. We knew our insurance would never let us go there, but we wanted a second opinion nonetheless.

Amber pressed on despite all the odds against her. In her final year of high school, she was on the Homecoming court, graduated in the top three percent of her high school class and garnished several scholarships toward her tuition at Cedarville University—the school she had wanted to attend since she was a little girl. The August before she packed up and left home, her FEV1 was down to twenty-eight percent.

Cedarville is where Amber's life changed forever. After the first few weeks of classes Amber had become so weak that she was unable to attend all of her lectures. Being the driven, conscientious student she had always been, she begged to stay, even after she was put on oxygen 24/7 in October of 2004.

She had no choice but to come home. Then, around Thanksgiving, after she met with Dr. Todd Astor at Columbus Children's Hospital, the Lord opened the door for an additional center in Ohio to be certified to perform double lung transplants. Upon meeting with Amber, Dr. Astor concluded that her condition had gone from serious to grave; she would need a double lung transplant within the next six to twelve months. As a family we came to terms with the truth: if Amber did not receive help—soon—she would die.

During her time at Cedarville, Amber began coming to terms with the harsh reality of a transplant as well. In her words, the Lord sent her on a journey—a fall that took everything she loved away from her and taught her that He must increase and she must decrease. Her pride was broken. After speaking from her heart to the entire Cedarville student body, she left the campus she loved in mid-December 2004.

From there, she went straight to Toledo Children's Hospital, where she had been treated since she was a baby, for yet another intense round of drugs. The goal was to salvage as much of her lungs as possible as we awaited Columbus Children's certification, the listing process, and ultimately the transplant.

For the next ten months, Amber had no choice but to rest—to rest in Him for everything, even breath itself. The days of our energetic daughter being the life of the party were over, but her relationship with Jesus Christ began to flourish.

In those long, heart-wrenching ten months, our beautiful Amber taught us more than we could ever have imagined. The way she lived her life taught us that when you walk with Christ, you can walk through your darkest hour and still have hope and joy. It was during this time that she became totally committed to allowing her life to be used however God saw fit. She taught us that when all you have is Jesus, He is enough. Obedience was a must for Amber and for our Christian lives in general. She planned her funeral, spent hours in her room with people who loved her and longed to see her get better, she sat at her computer and typed letters to hundreds of people when she could barely breathe, and she sang to her Savior with the assistance of oxygen. We did not know if Amber would live or die, but we did know that Amber loved the Lord and He was in control of it all.

Finally, on September 25, 2005, Amber received her double lung transplant and her recovery has been nothing short of breathtaking. We could never say thank you enough to the staff at Columbus Children's Medical Center for what they had done or to the countless people who prayed for and continue to pray for us. We do not take any of it lightly.

Amber does not have a clear bill of health, as transplant is not a cure for cystic fibrosis but rather a treatment. Sure, she is not at home as much as we would like, but it is a blessing to see our daughter living life and living it abundantly. She takes countless medications and visits the doctor regularly to check her blood work and lungs for rejection. Yet again, Amber has taken it all in stride. A year out of surgery, she is functioning like any normal person without cystic fibrosis, doing things only God can take credit for yet always aware that life is indeed a vapor and things could go horribly wrong in a very short amount of time.

The book title *Breathtaking* has a two-fold meaning for our family. Amber literally had her breath taken away, but God chose to give it back to her a hundredfold—not just for our pleasure but for His glory—and has allowed her to experience a dramatic recovery. God knew what she needed. Amber embraced the freedom of letting go and finding strength in Him and Him alone. She has confidence in who He has created her to be and she is answering this question: What am I going to do for God?

WHEN I THINK OF AMBER

It was a cold January morn
When into our home
Your love was born
And from day to day
God's light of love
Illuminates the way
And when the light
Begins to dim
He sends His angels
To work for Him
Offering words, kind and true,
We never doubt His
Love for you
It is His love that
Brings you to this day,
All grown up,
Ready to make your own way.
A daughter sent from Heaven,
A daughter to adore,
Today and every day
Since that cold January morn.
Love,

        Mom

Amber: We love you...
Love,

        Dad & Mom

JANUARY 1986–AUGUST 2004

Author's Note:

The following is a chronological medical timeline from birth to right before I left to attend Cedarville University. As time wore on, my cystic fibrosis began to take its toll. Every day before my transplant, I had to do two aerosol treatments a day, as well as chest therapy. My physicians always made sure I had the latest devices and medications to combat my disease, but despite all of the intervention, my cystic fibrosis continued to worsen.

- Born on January 2, 1986 weighing nine lbs. four ounces
- March 19, 1986: Diagnosed with cystic fibrosis
  — Was "failing to thrive" and had pulmonary disease present in lungs
  — Underwent a "sweat test" and was diagnosed with cystic fibrosis
  — Was hospitalized at Toledo Children's Hospital for approximately a month (five days in the ICU)
- 1989: The CF gene was discovered
  — Discovery of the gene has led to advancements in therapy
  — Sadly, still no cure for cystic fibrosis
- March of 1991: Performed first pulmonary function test
  — Results–79% FEC[3] & 84% FEV1[4]
- 1994–1999 (8-13 years of age)
  Yearly PFT[5] Results:
  — 1994 –95% FEC & 81% FEV1
  — 1995–86% FEC & 77% FEV1
  — 1996–71% FEC & 66% FEV1
  — 1997–86% FEC & 79% FEV1
  — 1998–64% FEC & 59% FEV1

- — 1999–52% FEC & 48% FEV1
- 2000-2004 (High School)
  - — January, 2002:
    - 65% FEC & 65% FEV1
    - Port inserted due to wearing out veins from years of IV therapy
  - — April, 2002 (after the musical)
    - 34% FEC & 31% FEV1 (Over a 30% drop in four months)
  - — After hospitalization that month:
    - 40% FEC & 35% FEV1
    - Referred to Cleveland Clinic for transplant evaluation
  - — January, 2003:
    - 37 % FEC & 31% FEV1
  - — December, 2003:
    - 30% FEC & 24% FEV1
  - — After hospitalization that month:
    - 30% FEC & 28% FEV1
    - Feeding tube inserted due to rapid weight loss and inability to get adequate nutrition; down to ninety-seven pounds.
  - — January, 2004:
    - 40% FEC & 29% FEV1
  - — May, 2004: High School Graduation
  - — July, 2004:
    - 37% FEC & 28% FEV1

Reflections

Lindsey:

In kindergarten there are no set criteria for who your best friends are going to be. You simply choose who you like, who you want to play with, and who looks like the most fun. You dash out to recess each afternoon, digging your heels into the cold, smooth pebbles scattered beneath the swings. You scan the playground for your loudest, most enthusiastic classmate, the one who makes you laugh and who pinky-swears that you'll be friends forever. The friendship is pure; there are no false motives, hidden agendas, or popularity contests. While you may envy their Jasmine doll or Creepy Crawlers kit, you certainly do not hold their good fortune against them as you know they will eventually let you borrow the desired toy "just for a little bit." You swap secrets, color pictures for one another, and even persuade your parents to write special passes for the bus drivers to drop you off at the other's house. You are convinced that your friendship is invincible and certain you will always be together. In kindergarten I had such a friend; and her name was Amber Metz.

Looking back, I don't remember how I responded when I discovered that Amber had a life-threatening illness. Frankly, I probably didn't care. Death doesn't seem a real possibility when you're six years old and, even if it did, Amber certainly didn't look ill. For me, Amber was Amber, not cystic fibrosis. We were friends and that was all that mattered.

As we grew older, however, it became more and more difficult to look past Amber's illness and the limitations it often imposed on her life. Not really understanding Amber's health condition, I would become frustrated with her for her inability—or what I believed was her unwillingness—to participate in all of the games in gym class and at recess. I distinctly remember how angry I became when she would bring in doctors' notes which excused her from certain fitness routines. I realize now that my anger was simply a façade I constructed to hide my fear of the severe implications of Amber's illness. All throughout elementary and middle school, I inwardly denied that Amber was any different from my other friends and classmates. It was as though I believed that if I denied that Amber's cystic fibrosis existed, it would eventually disappear. Problem solved—or so I thought.

In the fall of 2000, Amber and I entered our freshman year of high school, marking a new period both in our personal lives and in our friendship. During that year I finally began to acknowledge that Amber had a serious illness that was affecting far more than her inability to play dodge ball. More importantly, I began to notice how strong a role Amber's faith played in her life. While I was raised in the church and was a regular member of my high-school youth group, I realized that Amber had something in her faith that I had never experienced—complete assurance. She trusted God with her whole heart and was excited about what He was doing in her life. I remember thinking, "But I know all about God and go to church almost every week…how come I don't feel that same hope and excitement?" That was my problem—I knew God, but only with my head and not with my heart. While I could rattle off memory verses and parables, I never truly gave God my whole heart and life.

Although I did not realize it at the time, I am now certain that Amber was aware of my spiritual struggles and had been praying for me. It was no coincidence when she invited me to attend a local *Teens for Christ* meeting and I instantly felt a strong sense of purpose for being there. It certainly was no coincidence when, several months later, I dedicated my life to Christ in that very same *Teens for Christ* chapter.

While some people would like you to believe that God instantly promises to make your life easy the moment you come to know Him, there can be no statement further from the truth. My troubles did not disappear after I truly found Him, nor did Amber's cystic fibrosis vanish after she professed her faith when she was seven years old. What God does promise, however, is that He will never leave us to fight alone. The life I witnessed Amber leading throughout high school was a true testament to God's everlasting presence. Time and time again, Amber endured long visits to the hospital and was delivered devastating news of her deteriorating health. Amber's faith in God, however, was not weakened but strengthened in the face of adversity. This is not to say that she never became frustrated or angry with God, but that she never doubted His existence and His love for her. God never abandoned Amber, and Amber never abandoned God.

In August 2004, Amber and I packed our bags and our high-school lives and departed for college. Although our two universities were only twenty minutes apart from one another, the distance might as well have been three hundred miles. I struggled with the transition to college and missed everything and everyone who had been a part of my high school life. Ironically, I dealt with my problems by cutting myself off from those I was closest to; I simply didn't want to face that they had moved on and that I would need to as well. Thus, I was largely unaware of how poor Amber's health had become during the first few months of college. In November I visited Amber at Cedarville and saw how tired she looked and how frail she had become. I realized then that Amber would not be able to make it much longer at Cedarville and that she was in desperate need of either a transplant or a miracle. (As I later came to realize, a transplant in itself is a miracle.)

After seeing Amber on that cold November evening, I vowed to become a better friend and not to allow my own insecurities to cut me off from those I love. While I cannot say that I always held true to that promise (Amber can attest that my first reaction is always to close up when I am struggling), I slowly began to reconnect with Amber and rebuild our close friendship. Over the course of the next ten months, I watched as Amber's health deteriorated and our friendship grew stronger. I long ago lost count of the number of evenings I spent with Amber at her house, either listening to music or just talking. Although we could rarely leave the house, we got into the habit of loading Amber and her oxygen tanks into the car, cranking up the volume on the radio, and driving out into the open country to chase the sun as it edged beneath the horizon. Those late summer evenings with Amber yelling "Follow that sun!" are now some of my best memories of what was an otherwise tense time.

It was not until September, 2005 that Amber received the news that we had all been waiting for—a pair of lungs was available and she was at the top of the transplant list. As the news spread, excitement turned to chaos; I probably drove Amber crazy with the number of times I called her asking when she was going into surgery and when I should arrive at the hospital. After what seemed like hours, my friend and former teacher, Heather Harmon, arrived to pick me up at my college, and we began the drive to Columbus Children's Hospital. Looking back on the evening and the eleven-hour surgery, I don't ever remember feeling nervous—excited, but never nervous. I simply remember thinking that the surgery was in God's hands and that the result, whether positive or negative, would be His will. Amber wouldn't want it any other way.

Needless to say, Amber survived her surgery and had a miraculous recovery. She is once again the Amber I met on that dusty playground in 1991—loud, energetic, and full of life and laughter. However, she displays a greater sensitivity, boldness, and willingness to glorify God than I ever remember that six-year-old having. Her many years of physical ailments and her struggle for survival have made her a stronger person, both spiritually and emotionally. God allowed Amber to have cystic fibrosis for a reason, and she used—and continues to use—her struggles for His glory. Although Amber has received her transplant, her spiritual journey is far from over; rather, it has just begun. Amber's tale is not a story of overcoming death—it is a story of finding life.

CHAPTER THREE

Broken

Cedarville University is where the Lord brought me to my knees and began the refinement process that has made me the young woman I am today. As I continue to walk the path the Lord has laid out before me, I continue to be reminded of my time at Cedarville. As I told the entire study body the Friday before I left: "Let go and trust Him. Love Him–that's all He's asking of you." Cedarville was where I learned to fly into my loving Father's arms and leave behind the fears that fettered my soul.

"The barbarian way is not about violence fueled by vengeance and hatred. The barbarian way is about love expressed through sacrifice and servant hood...When you join the barbarian tribe, you begin to live your life with your eyes and your heart wide open. When the Spirit of God envelops your soul, your spirit comes alive, and everything changes for you. You are no longer the same. And to those who cannot see the invisible, to those who refuse to believe it exists, the path you choose, the life you live, may lead them to conclude that you are not simply different but insane. People who are fully alive look out of their minds to those who simply exist."

—Erwin McManus[6]

Author's Note:

*T*his is the email I sent to update all the teachers at Wapakoneta High School on my condition and plans to return home from college. I graduated from Wapakoneta Senior High School on May 29, 2004:

DECEMBER 14, 2004:

WHS Faculty:

I'm sure you all remember me–and if you don't, shame on you! It has been a long time since I had a few of you in class, but please know you haven't been forgotten. I appreciate all of you, and I want to let you in on some things that have been going on with me since I came to Cedarville University this past fall.

First of all, I hope your holiday season hasn't been too stressful and that your students are being good to you. You only have a few more days until break! All of you remember my ongoing health condition and the various difficulties I faced during high school, particularly my sophomore and senior years. I was bound and determined to make it to college, though, and God blessed me with the drive to fight through everything and still succeed in school. I was able to come to Cedarville almost debt-free, and I was very excited about the next four years. I enrolled in a program that seemed tailored especially for me. My major in

Comprehensive Communications and minors in Bible, Psychology, and Women's ministries fit me perfectly. I couldn't have been happier. (Yes, I know that sounds like a lot. It *is* me, though.) God had different plans, however, and by the end of September I was getting worn out faster than usual. I knew something was up. I went home for fall break in the middle of October, and at that time I still felt pretty decent. I hadn't missed a lot of class, and I was still keeping up with my 17.0 credit hour schedule. By the end of October, though, I was placed on portable liquid oxygen 24/7 and my health continued to fail me. I was missing more lectures, and there were days I stayed in bed the entire day. You all know me, and you know Amber doesn't stay in bed. There wasn't really anything anyone could do for me, though, considering I have CF. You can't just give me some antibiotics and expect everything to go away.

I went home over Thanksgiving break to find out that my lung capacity was down to nineteen percent (under sixteen percent depending on what measurements you use[7]) and the upper lobes of my lungs had collapsed. The only option I have now is a transplant, and according to Columbus Children's Medical Center, where I'll have the procedure done, that should be within the next six to twelve months. They technically don't have their center up and running yet, so my parents and I are playing everything by ear. We know God has brought this center out of the blue for a reason. My parents and I have never been impressed with Cleveland Clinic–where I've gone the past two years to be evaluated. My insurance will not allow me to go to North Carolina or Pittsburgh, two of the top centers in the nation. I have to stay around here, and Columbus is where I want to go. The new center should be up and running (hopefully) by March, and at that time they should list me. After that, the wait isn't too terribly long. They don't want to list me, though, until they absolutely have to, considering the surgery is so taxing and it's not a cure; transplants usually last eight to ten years.

I will also be in the Toledo Hospital from Dec. 18th to Jan. 7th. The goal is to get IVs in me and get me stabilized. Obviously, my life has been turned upside down, but I know God is in complete control. I'm not giving up hope at all. I have made the decision, with the advice of my doctors, to leave Cedarville after this semester, go home to take classes online, and get the proper care I need. I will be taking online courses in counseling and other ministry-related issues from Moody Bible Institute for next semester. I will return to Cedarville after my transplant, if the Lord wills. If not, I'll be doing something else. Money and degrees truly don't make the world go around. It's all about perspective and finding out what really matters in life.

I've bought a computer/desk/chair, picked a new school, and signed the papers needed to get out of Cedarville all in the past twelve days. Life has certainly been shoved into the fast lane. I am totally at peace about it all, though, and I know God has a plan. I knew you all would want to know. I cherish the time I had at WHS, and there are nights I lie in my bed wishing I could go back to when life was simpler. Lindsey Short and I were discussing how we truly didn't understand how good we had it back in high school; it all seems so long ago. I didn't email you all to depress you. I wanted to encourage you. God is good, and even when we cannot see ahead, He does. May your holiday season be one of joy and peace.

God bless,
Amber N. Metz-2004 WHS graduate

Author's Note:

This e-mail was sent out the morning I left Cedarville University and came home to embrace the unknown:

DECEMBER 15, 2004

Cedarville University–"Thank you" could never convey…

I knew I'd have to write this entry, and I've been dreading it. I would much rather return to all of you next semester perfectly healthy and ready to actually go to class! God has other plans, though. I do promise you that if He wants me back here in the future, I'll be here in a heartbeat. I love all of you so much, and I can't begin to express how even the little things have touched me over the semester. You all say how much I've made an impact on you, but I cannot tell you how much of a blessing it is to walk alongside such encouraging, strong brothers and sisters in Christ.

I wish I could go to each one of you and tell you how much you mean to me, but you all must rest assured that you will not be forgotten, and the impact you've had on me will be forever stamped on my life. My time here at Cedarville was not in vain and I know God brought me here to strip me down to nothing and show me who He *really* is. Let me tell you, He's amazing. He's my Everything. He wants you, too. My prayer for you, Cedarville, is two words:

LET GO

…of everything: your hopes, your dreams, and your ambitions. Allow Him to have free reign in your life, and I promise you–I *promise* you-you won't regret it. You can bet the farm on it; you can even bet your life on it. He can use y'all in ways I could never be used. Happiness isn't in degrees or future bank accounts, it's in Him and the promises He gave us in His Word. We win, people; let's start acting like it!

It's 2:23 A.M. I have nothing packed, and I'm sitting here crying…I'm not surprised. Once a procrastinator always a procrastinator, right? All my love and prayers to *all* of you.

Goodnight, Cedarville…

DECEMBER 2004–JANUARY 2005

- Left Cedarville University on December 15, 2004
- Spent Christmas, New Year's and my 19th birthday in Toledo Children's Hospital
- Still on oxygen therapy
- 24% FEC & 16% FEV1-Toledo's numbers
- Awaited Columbus Children's Medical Center's certification as a licensed lung-transplant center

Cedarville Reflections:

Garret:

Amber is an odd person when you really get to know her—and don't take that as a negative statement because it's not. She is just not one of those people of whom you can say, "Oh, she is one of those"; there is not a group she fits in. She is herself, and to try and explain her by describing her as a combination of this person and that person would do her no justice. I have not always known her in this way, though, and as I sit here during my junior year of college, I realize I have only known her for about three years. But I feel as though she has become one of my closest friends.

In my senior year of high school I joined this traveling ministry team which is a part of a local jr. high/high school ministry, *Teens for Christ*. She had been on the team the previous year as well, and during our senior year she was the leader of the women in the group. I got to know her after opening up about her disease had become easier for her; it was so sad to hear about it. She would talk about the odds of her surviving to see age thirty-five, and said that eventually she would need a transplant. She told us all that a transplant would most likely last ten years or so, so she was hoping to hold out until she was twenty-five to get one.

The team we were on was serious about seeking the Lord and giving all of our life to Him, yet her devotion was different; she didn't know how much time she had on earth and so she didn't want to wait to really start living for God's glory and His kingdom. She was all about being real and authentic, and when she started opening up and sharing about not only her disease but her heart for Jesus, it shocked people into reality. For her it was simple (but not easy) to put off all the games and be serious about dying to herself and following Christ because she was constantly reminded about how frail her life was and that it could end at any second.

But isn't our life just the same? Our world is just as unsafe; people die in freak accidents or random murders all the time. Shouldn't we live the same way as Amber? I think Jesus said something about not getting too focused on our plans for life and worrying about the future but to live for each day and to seek His kingdom first. Her testimony made people think, "If this little girl isn't going to live to my age and she is full of such passion for the Lord, shouldn't I be the same? What about all the time I have wasted so far?"

I hope I am not making her come across as insincere and as a Christian Nazi, but unless you are around her, it is hard to describe the fire inside her that burns to see God's name lifted up. She did (and still does) really care about people, maybe even a little too much. She is slowly losing her lung capacity, but all she can think about is the fact that her friends are hurting and need love.

Continuing with the story, that year on the ministry team was great and every one on that team grew close; it was great community. Things did get a little complicated though. When high school boys and girls get around each other for a long time, it turns into a Christian soap opera. Amber liked my best friend and I liked her best friend. Unfortunately, like all standard Emo songs, we all graduated and parted ways, though we still had feelings for these people.

Amber and I ended up going to Cedarville University and this was where I got to know Amber in all of her weakness, and she got to know me in all of mine. Both of us ended up being crushed by other people. It felt like chunks of my heart kept falling into the pit of my stomach and sat there rotting. At that time I needed someone to talk to, and Amber was the only one available who knew the whole situation. For a guy to call a girl and admit that not only is he hurt but needs someone to talk to is one of the most humbling things in the world. Amber was also really hurt and, for some reason, God loves to use relationships to tear us apart so that He can do a work in us that is just between us and Him. That situation would have to be the one that brought us the closest. It was good to know someone cared about me and didn't want me to be sad and upset. She still had trouble with the one guy she had feelings for, and what made it worse was that she was getting weaker.

By the end of the semester, she was so weak and ghastly thin. She skipped many classes and it was a rarity to see her in chapel. Even though she was not that active, she was becoming more and more known around campus. She sent out emails about how she was feeling and the things she was doing; people talked about her all the time. I guess wherever she goes she ends up having an effect on people, or maybe it is because she can't stop talking. Either way, God really used her then (and now) to speak to people.

She is a real person whom God had allowed everything in her life that brought her comfort to be taken away. Nothing was left to sustain her but God Himself. She came to Cedarville with just under thirty percent of her lung capacity, and all the walking and cold weather had taken its toll on her. Her lung capacity was about twenty percent by the time she left to go home for Christmas.

The next semester passed by. She stayed at home and we kept in contact. It was a lonely time for her, but then summer finally came and all her friends came home. The summer was an interesting experience with all of her equipment and oxygen tanks. I am pretty sure all of her friends are now certified professionals of oxygen materials and maintenance.

Time flew by and we all had to pack up and go back to school. About a month later, Amber got the call to have her surgery. Carla and I drove from Cedarville to Columbus in record time. We were fortunate to see her right before she went into surgery. At the time, I didn't feel like I was possibly saying goodbye to my friend. It didn't hit me that the last memory I might have had would have been worship music and strawberry-scented anesthetic.

After they wheeled her into surgery we went up to a waiting room, and prayed, and tried to do things to busy ourselves, but it didn't work. Every once in a while the doctors would come in and let us know what was going on, and then that the organs looked great.

Eventually morning came and we had that too-worried-to-be-tired feeling, the fake-awake feeling. We went and got breakfast in the cafeteria, though food was the last thing on our minds.

Around 10 or 11 A.M., they finished and told us the surgery had gone well, and that we might even get to see her before we left. In the end, only her family was allowed to go in, but thanks to digital cameras we saw what she looked like. It was a sight I will never forget. There were so many tubes and machines and instruments on this frail little girl, it seemed like something from a movie. But thanks to the genius of a bunch of people and of course the favor of God, Amber came through the surgery. Recovery for her was off the charts, which just seemed like something Amber would do.

Life has changed so much for her since then. She went from being too weak to get out of bed to not wanting to get any sleep at all. Now we see a girl with more odds against her than most people have. But in spite of it all, she is living this amazing life.

Amber started believing in who God says she is and in what He has called her to do. This is no different for any one of us.

Why would God redeem us with the ultimate price of His Son's life only to have us simply go to church once a week? Did He run out of things that need to be done? What would He say: "Well, Jim, um…basically all my slots are full. I know the entire world needs to be saved, and countless children are hungry, and poverty and hopelessness rule the world, but I've got nothing for you today. Come back next week and I will see if something opens up"? But, I am no one great, we say. Exactly! No one is great. That's why He uses the weak and despised things of this world to shame the people that think they have it all together. He gets glory.

I am not saying that all of us will become famous, because fame is fleeting and will be swallowed up by time. We will remember only a few names from countless ages of history; names, friends, love, sadness, distress—all are lost in time. Many things in life are vanity, so we are to find our place in the body and work for something that will last. That way we can all work together to spread the name of Jesus, so that He will be worshipped by the entire world. Amber dreams big, and right now she is not yet well known. But we will see what happens. Whatever that may be, though, may it be a testimony to each one that God is big and He can do more than we could ever imagine.

Carla:

Amber and I had spent nearly a year together in a ministry called *Teens for Christ* before we realized that we had both decided, quite apart from each other, to attend Cedarville University. During that year, Amber and I had been very cordial to each other, but that was about the extent of our friendship; she was dating a guy who had liked me—one of those situations. And Amber was much more outgoing than me—the stand-on-the-table-and-give-a-speech-at-your-birthday-party kind of outgoing. I was more reserved. Funny how I've learned that the very "extrovertness" I found intimidating is actually one of Amber's strengths.

So when we realized that we were going to be living in the same unit at Cedarville, I was a little nervous. My birthday was during the first week of classes. Was she going to make me get up on a table in the cafeteria and give a speech? Ahhh!! Thankfully, my birthday passed without incident. Actually, our living in the same unit turned out not only to be a good thing but also a God thing. I have no doubt whatsoever that God put us together during that semester to grow closer and to remind each other that we were not alone during those very dark days.

Some of the good memories that I have include learning to play money-free poker with Murray, Garret, Jesse and Roy; stuffing many Oreos in our mouths during open dorms; making runs to Mom and Dad's for chicken wraps, and long talks by the lake.

Ahhh, those long talks by the lake. Taking a walk around the Cedarville "lake" is said to be one of the most romantic things to do on campus: the soft glow of the buildings on the surface, the feel of the wind as it whips off the bridge and the layers of green moss that gather all around the shore, yum. To be quite honest, I don't find moss terribly romantic, but the lake did provide the perfect place for Amber and me to have some pretty serious discussions that semester. We talked about her health, what it meant to really follow Jesus, and a lot about one specific boy. It was during these boy conversations in particular that I realize that I, introvert Carla, had something of importance to say to extrovert Amber. "Don't emotionally date him; you broke up, you know." "Don't talk to him for a while; give yourself some space. If he's the kind of guy I know he is, then he'll understand."

In the midst of out conversations, I was learning some very important things too: That there really is a time to be silent and a time to speak; That it's ok to admit that I have problems, if they're really my friends, they'll still love me. Out-of-control circumstances (i.e. Amber's health) can actually be blessings because they give us an opportunity to stretch our trust in God.

Amber's health changed quite dramatically during the months that we were at Cedarville. She had arrived full of energy and ready to take on the whole campus. As time went by, and the weather got colder, she slowly began to lose her stamina and energy. As long as I had known her, Amber had used an oxygen machine in the privacy of her own home/dorm room. But that semester, when we went home for Thanksgiving break, Amber's doctor told her that she had to use the oxygen all the time. So after Thanksgiving, a huge machine with compressed oxygen for Amber's portable tank came to live in our closet. Looking back now, I can see how Amber always tried to make light of her health situation, which was obviously very serious. When she had to be on oxygen all the time, she joked that it was really just a ploy to sneak men into the dorm; a guy had to come by about once a week to fill the compressed oxygen tank. As long as I've known her, Amber has always been like that, looking for the good, looking for a way to give God the glory. I think that's why she recovered so well after the surgery—her attitude of not taking things too seriously and her utter confidence that God would do what was best.

The last three weeks of her semester at Cedarville were awful. I don't think she went to more than two classes the whole time. She was too sick to make the trek to the cafeteria to eat so I would often go across the street to get her a chicken wrap and sweet tea from Mom and Dad's. Her parents and even her doctor wanted her to come home, and I thought she would be better off at home, too. But Amber was determined to stick it out and stay for the whole term. She got the opportunity to give a short testimony in one of the last chapels and our unit prayed for her in front of the whole student body. We also had a good-bye party, so friends could say more personal good-byes. Amber was such a good faker when she was really sick. At her party, she was smiley and bouncy, but as soon as the last person left she wilted and had to stay in bed for quite a while.

When I returned to school the next semester, it was so different to be there with no Amber. In a way, I was very relieved that she was home where she could be better taken care of and where hopefully she wouldn't deteriorate as fast. But in another way it was very sad too, and I was almost angry with God. Why did such a horrible thing have to happen to such a wonderful girl? It was so unfair that she couldn't live a normal life like any other 19-year-old. Sometimes I still struggle with these questions, but I always have to come back to the foundation of what I believe by faith, that God is good, He does love us, and He's trying to use the hard things in our lives to conform us more into the image of His Son, if only we will respond correctly.

I think those truths are some of the most important things that I've learned on this journey with Amber. This journey hasn't been easy, and I know there are harder times yet to come. But God has challenged me to trust Him more, especially in the hard times, and when I respond correctly, I know He uses those hard circumstances to form me more into the image of Jesus. That doesn't make hard situations easy but it puts them in a little better perspective. It's as James says:

"Consider it pure joy, my brothers and sisters, whenever you face trials of many kinds, because you know that the testing of your faith produces perseverance. Let perseverance finish its work so that you may be mature and complete, not lacking anything" James 1:2-4 (NIV). It's an honor to know Amber, and I'm so glad that God has let us take this journey together and with everyone else.

Julie:

I met Amber about three weeks before she had to leave Cedarville due to her rapidly declining health. Later I wrote in my journal about the nights I spent with Amber before she left. It started off as a simple visit to her unit to see a mutual friend and, as night turned into morning, I lay next to her in bed holding her hand and hugging her as we laughed and cried sharing each other's life stories. It was during those few precious nights before she left a couple of weeks later that we would share our dreams, our desires, our hearts, our struggles, our Jesus. A friendship began which only God could have woven together in such a short period of time. I came back one night and wrote in my journal:

> 12/12/04 3:21 A.M.
> "No guilt in life, no fear in death,
> This is the power of Christ in me.
> From life's first cry to final breath
> Jesus commands my destiny.
> No power of hell, no scheme of man
> Can ever pluck me from His hand.
> 'Til He returns or calls me home,
> Here in the power of Christ I'll stand"[8]
> Amber has been the angel who has showed me what it means
> to live.

I have watched Amber face battle after battle head-on and claim victory through Jesus Christ's power in her life. To Him she gives all glory and honor, and to Him she lives and breathes each moment of each day. She will be the first to admit that she isn't perfect, that there were days she wanted to give up, that the fight seemed too long, lonely and draining. But it was on those days that the power of Christ was displayed through her, for as it states in 2 Cor. 12:9, "My grace is sufficient for you, for my power is made perfect in weakness." She knew that fight, those days of loneliness, of sickness, of struggle, was going to be worth it because she was living for someone and something higher than herself. She has lived out what it means to find joy in suffering, to find hope in desperation, to find unconditional love in the only One who can provide what some of us spend our whole lives searching for. She so much desires that the rest of us find what she has in our heavenly Father, that freedom of running the race not for earthly things or for ourselves, but for the much higher and eternal calling of serving our Lord and Savior Jesus Christ.

The Lord has blessed me and showed me so much of Himself through my friendship with Amber. I have been blessed with a friend who, after talking to her for five minutes or five hours, makes me want to go run and spend time with my heavenly Father. Amber won't let me settle for any less than to desire Him and crave Him and believe that He can do anything through me because He is God and I am not. Amber won't let you settle for any less. I have a friend who pushes me toward Jesus. All to say, to have a friend that pushes you towards Jesus the way she does...well is to have an angel as a friend.

I love you my CU angel...

FEBRUARY-MARCH 2005

Before I was listed on the
United Network of Organ Sharing (U.N.O.S)

- 21% FEV1 by Columbus Children's measurements
- On 2.0-2.5 L of oxygen
- Discontinued my coursework with Moody Bible Institute, due to my failing health
- Columbus Children's certified as a transplant center
- Planned my funeral with my family and close friends on March 6, 2005
- Continued follow-up with Columbus, preparing to be listed for transplant on the United Network of Organ Sharing's (U.N.O.S) national list by the end of March 2005
- Tests that were performed in order to be on the list were as follows:
  1. Chest radiography
  2. CT of chest, abdomen, and sinuses.
  3. VQ nuclear med scan
  4. Bone density
  5. Echocardiogram
  6. Electrocardiogram
  7. Pulmonary function tests with DLCO, pre-& post-bronchodilator
  8. Psychosocial consult/assessment
  9. Pulmonary rehab consult
  10. ENT consult
  11. Vial upon vial of blood taken for numerous tests
  12. Synergy studies

Let's just say, a LOT of tests/studies!

At the end of March, I had sinus surgery, which ended up with my having complications.

MARCH 20, 2005:

I'm so thankful to be sitting here still among all of you. I know a lot of you haven't heard yet, but I had quite the scare on Thursday. To make a long, scary story as short as possible: I had sinus surgery Tuesday (which went perfectly fine.) I was on the road to recovery until Thursday morning when my nose decided it was going to bleed, and bleed, and bleed some more. After fifteen hours, two ERs, a car ride to Columbus that felt like it was going to kill me, tracking down my surgeon at midnight, and more blood than I've ever seen, everything *finally* was under control. I just have this thing jammed up my nose until tomorrow when I go back to Columbus to have it removed. Dr. Willet, my surgeon, said that if I start bleeding again, he has another remedy. Let's just pray we don't have to try something else.

Thursday was probably the worst day of my life. I would take not being able to breathe over not being able to breathe *and* choking on my own blood *any* day. I laugh about it now, but it wasn't funny then.

I woke up Friday morning so upset with myself, knowing that I could have had better control of my actions. Bringing God glory wasn't exactly my number one priority throughout that awful day. But I've been reminded that I am indeed human, and that's *OK.* God knows I love Him more than anything in this fallen world. I'm just glad He didn't take me Home on Thursday because that's not how I would have wanted to go out.

All I know is, God's in control and He has blessed me with *so* much. I have grown so much closer to Him through this whole ordeal, and I know it's *far* from over. Transplant is a long, hard road, and I know the ones closest to me cannot wait until we've crossed a few more bridges and have some more experiences under our belt.

Reflections

John:

Some things in life you never expect. Some of those are good, some aren't. Some are just, well, unexpected. I think everyone has, at some point in his life, wondered what he would do if he had a terminal disease. I don't think many have wondered what they would do if a friend had a terminal disease. Not that the disease itself is unexpected—it's part of Amber; we all know that. But I never expected that I would be so close to someone with cystic fibrosis and see a disease I'd hardly heard of affect my life in so many ways.

I met Amber through a friend. It started as an "IM friendship"—middle schoolish, I know, but we were only sophomores. When I met Amber, I met CF—cystic fibrosis. So we wound up as "boyfriend and girlfriend" that summer. Well, for two weeks anyway. The first time she went into a coughing spell around me, I didn't know what to do. I couldn't fix it, and I didn't know how to react. So I pretty much just sat there.

I wound up having a lot more contact with Amber. Doing ministry together has that effect. By the end of our junior year of high school we were dating, a little more for real this time, but we were still just kids. Dating a girl with CF is an adventure. Or, maybe, just dating Amber is an adventure. Maybe Amber is just an adventure. But a guy dating Amber has some different things to remember than the average "Joe Boyfriend": she likes peach roses and doesn't like chocolate, long romantic walks are out of the question, she must be reminded to take her enzymes before meals—half a dozen pills or more–and one tends to keep in mind the nearest hospital and quickest way to get there, just in case. It's easy to take her breath away, though. Sorry, bad joke.

It also meant that I saw more than a lot of people. She tried to hide a lot from me, but when you're with someone that much, it's hard. She hated being weak, but I saw her in her weakness more than once. But it didn't slow her down, ever. I am proud to have done ministry with her; she's fierce and she pushes us all. In all her strength, though, it was hard to watch my girlfriend unable to breathe, knowing I could do nothing. A man's instinct is to fix things, especially for those about whom he cares. I got used to the coughing spells. I learned just to wait them out, but I hated waiting and I always wondered if this was the time I was going to have to find out how quickly I could weave that T-bird through downtown traffic.

After about eleven months God made it clear to me that Amber was not the girl He intended me to marry. It was a gut-wrenching decision. The CF was getting worse, and I didn't know how to make it clear that the disease hadn't scared me off. Then we graduated. I went to college in Georgia, and suddenly I was 500 miles from everyone I knew, including Amber. I fell out of contact with everyone. Not that I went antisocial, I just suddenly realized that I was a really bad communicator when I didn't see people on a regular basis. It was hard but it was good for me, and God taught me a lot about myself. But there were friends back home who needed me, including Amber. And I wasn't there.

Amber was getting worse; we knew she needed the transplant. My friends were aghast that I barely seemed to care. I did, more than I could tell them. But God did something amazing for me, I guess, because He knew I needed reassurance from Him. I don't know how, or why, but God always made it clear to me that Amber would be OK, at least for now. The transplant would come, and would succeed. Not that it would be painless, but it would be OK. He didn't tell me this audibly one day, or write it in the clouds or the fog on my bathroom mirror, He didn't show me a vision of the future. I just knew. It was a peace I can't explain. But that peace and my own tendencies to try to be the immovable, emotionless tower of strength unfortunately gave friends that I didn't talk to nearly enough the impression that I was unfazed by Amber's illness.

Then I came back for spring break, and Amber told me that she was getting us all together—to plan her funeral. Now let's lay down the rest of the background: first we have the assurance from God, so I honestly had no belief that Amber was going to die. Beyond that there is the awkwardness between two people who used to date. We always hope it won't happen to you, and we always say that it won't. We always say that the old friendship will pick up where we left it off if we break up. But it doesn't. It dissipates in time, but the awkwardness always sets in. It's stupid, but it's life. Two strikes. Then of course there were all these friends who felt as though they'd gotten the shaft from me, even though I loved them all more than I can say. Strike three and I'm out. But I was there anyway, and we planned a funeral. It was one of the most awkward, uncomfortable, depressing activities of my life. Amber's dad was sitting right there with us; I can only imagine how he felt.

Amber has a favorite hymn, and I share it with her. After losing all four of his daughters in a shipwreck, Horatio Gates Spafford wrote, "Whatever my lot, Thou hast taught me to say 'It is well, it is well with my soul.'"[8] That's a hymn of Amber's life. Sorrows have rolled like sea billows, and her lot has not been pleasant. But God has used her. He continues to use her—powerfully. She throws herself into following Him and serving Him. No, she's not perfect; she has her hang-ups as we all do, but her passion and fervor are unmatched. Amber asked me to sing that song at the funeral we planned. We didn't use those plans this time, but they're sealed up in an envelope somewhere and I expect I'll sing it eventually. I guarantee that this "rock" of a guy won't make it through without bawling. But that time isn't now, so I will rejoice in this young woman's friendship and ministry. And however this all goes down, you know what? It's still well.

EARLY APRIL 2005

- Had been home from Cedarville for four months
- Had just begun writing emails to close friends and family
- 21% FEV1
- On 2.5 L of oxygen twenty-four hours a day
- Completed all the necessary requirements to be listed
- Still waiting to be listed, after being told I would be on the United Network of Organ Sharing by the end of March

CHAPTER FOUR

Surrender through Transparency

While becoming transparent with others and, more importantly, with my Lord, I found myself letting go of the façade and embracing the fact that through my weakness *He* was made strong (2 Cor. 12:9). Everything I held dear (my health, my friends, my future, my desires, etc.) was lost in order to gain my greatest treasure–freedom in Christ. I didn't care if I lived or died; I just wanted more of Him.

"Some people come into our lives and quickly go.
Others stay awhile and leave footprints on our heart and we are never the same."

—Anonymous

APRIL 3, 2005-DEMO

*T*here's a problem in Christianity today. Being "real" has been tossed out for everyone wearing a facade. I know, because I wore one for many, many years. If I'm not careful, it's very easy for me to go into my closet, find an old mask, and go back to how I used to be.

We sit around in our Christian circles and talk about the Final Four, HALO, and even the weather. When it comes to getting down to brass tacks, though, we squirm. If someone were to ask us how we're doing spiritually, we have this universal answer: "Oh, I'm all right. How 'bout you?" It's almost as though we're acting, like we're passing some stranger on the street who just said, "Hey, how's your day going?," and we reply out of obligation and common courtesy. Let's be serious here. How many of us are even being real with *ourselves* when it comes to how we're doing spiritually/emotionally/mentally? Maybe we've suppressed how we really feel for so long that we honestly couldn't tell someone how we are even if we tried. We think we know, but we have no idea. I know because that's how I was.

If we can't be real with *ourselves*, how do we *ever* expect to be vulnerable with others? I'm here to say that it is *so* vital to our Christian life to be able to stand up and admit when we need help. If we can't fall flat on our faces before people we can see and admit we're struggling, how are we going to be able to talk to God about it? We may mutter something to Him now and then about it, but I'm talking about gut-wrenching, pouring-your-heart-out, tears-dripping-down-your-face, confessing-your-need-for-your-Savior talk. So once we're willing to be real with God and ourselves, that's when others come into the picture. There's a problem in that, though. Being real isn't exactly the thing to do in the church, or so it seems. We walk into church and we immediately put our smile on, just like the other people there. Walk into some services, and we'd think the whole congregation had spent their entire life at Disney World—everyone's just so "happy." When we ask sweet Ms. Betty how she's doing, and she says, "Oh, I'm wonderful," don't be surprised if she's just been diagnosed with terminal cancer and has six months to live.

How are we different than the world if we can't even come alongside our brothers and sisters and meet them where they are? We, as the body of Christ, can't even seem to get the guts up to talk about the *real* issues. For example, if you are in college, maybe someone in the dorm is struggling with anorexia, self-mutilation, pornography, masturbation or thoughts of suicide, but they feel that they can't tell anyone. After all, what would they *think?* We've already decided that they wouldn't understand. I would just like to say I'm sorry. I'm sorry for anyone who has been fed the lie that vulnerability shows weakness, that there's no one out there who would get it. I do know one thing: No matter what's in our past, what we've done or what we're struggling with, **He loves us** and He's more than willing to heal us. We have to make the first step, though, and it's going to hurt. We can't do it alone either. Find accountability. If you feel like you've been pushed away, find someone else.

The world isn't looking for our passion plays, pretty churches, or snow camps. They just want us to be *real,* to show that we serve a *living* God and not pretend to have it all together. We aren't any better than them. We've just been blessed beyond measure to know a risen Savior. We *have* the answers, so why are we hiding behind our facades so we can look as good as possible?

I'm done wearing a mask. I'm done sugarcoating my life and how I feel. I screw up, but I'm not going to sit here in mediocrity and act as if it's no big deal. I've been hurt, lied to, beat up, abused, and rejected just as all of us have. We all have ghosts in our closet, and sometimes it takes years and years to get them out. God loves us, though, so much and He's waiting for our lead. It's time we meet and start walking on the road less traveled.

APRIL 5, 2005-PRIDE

I had to make a compromise today. What I really wanted to do was go drive down a familiar road at sunset, with the windows rolled down and my hair blowing in the wind. I was talked out of that, though. So I did the next best thing; I went to the backyard. I tore my closet apart looking for some summer clothes, grabbed my oxygen, my Bible, my journal, a pen, book, phone, and the radio.

My favorite part of the whole thing was the wind. It was as if God was wrapping His arms around me, letting me know He was there. I see the tree outside my window every day, and I see the effects of the wind on the branches all the time. There's just something about feeling it for myself, though—being the branch, if you will.

I want to be (and am) the branch in a lot of ways. I want to be pruned for my own good. I want to be stripped down to the bare minimum, made a fool in the eyes of men; I want to sacrifice and struggle. It seems that it takes our being stripped down to nothing to realize how much we desperately *need* Him. Why does it have to be this way? Why can't we see it as clear as day from day one? Why do we have to be so *disgustingly* prideful? After all of our energy and plans are exhausted *then* we turn to Him; He's like our last resort.

Life isn't a business. God is not the CEO who comes out on the floor maybe once a year to visit the workers on the line just for good PR. Imagine this: Jesus walks up to a man working on the engine of a car. The man seems to be having some difficulty getting the parts connected properly. He doesn't seem to have the proper tools. Jesus says, "Good afternoon, sir. How's it going?" The frustrated worker immediately recognizes who he's talking to, so he tries to hide any sense of nervousness. Putting his best face forward, and acting as if the engine is coming along smoothly, He says, "Mr. Jesus, it's a pleasure to see you, sir. Thank you so much for that five-cent raise last year. You're the best boss ever." Jesus turns and acts as if He's leaving, so the man rushes back to his work. Jesus turns back around, puts his arm around the man, and slips the wrench the man so desperately needed into his other hand.

Sometimes no matter how much we *think* we have all that it takes, we don't. We aren't supposed to, either. He wants to be an *active* part of our walk; He's the reason *for* our walk! We need to lay down our pride. If we have to, we lay it down, run it over with a semi a few times, and then fall flat on our face before our Father in Heaven—tire marks and all. He's waiting. We get so caught up in what we think we deserve—the questions that don't have answers, the questions that have answers that we don't like, and the feelings of insecurity and insufficiency that plague us all at one point or another.

So, yes, I saw the sunset tonight. It wasn't as grand and glorious as it would have been driving down a country road, but it made me smile. It made me feel small and vulnerable compared to my big God, and that's just the way I like it.

APRIL 10, 2005-NO EXCUSES

I'm tired of making excuses, of hearing excuses. I make *way* too many sometimes. If God says go, GO. There are some things that we sit around and contemplate as being the will of God when the answer is quite clear. We are to love the Lord with all of our heart, mind, and soul—that's a *command,* not an option. It requires daily sacrifice, sweat, blood, and tears. We are called to **GO** and make disciples of all nations, baptizing them in the name of the Father and the Son and the Holy Spirit (Matthew 28:19-20). We don't have to sit around and wonder about whether or not we should sacrifice it all every day for Him or profess His name and His works to others. Those are present-tense imperatives. They applied 2000 years ago, and they still apply today.

Mediocrity is so evident in the Church as a whole. Christians are some of the best self-lawyers I've ever seen. We try to justify our actions to God, always pointing out what the other guy has and hasn't been doing. It's not about *them*. It's about *us* and God. God is personal. We all relate to and worship Him differently, as we should. After all, *no one* on this earth can worship Him the way *that each of us as individuals* can. Our relationship with Jesus Christ brings the Father glory, glory that is personal and unique because it's a reflection of His work in each individual life.

It says in the Word, "And that slave who knew his master's will and did not get ready or act in accord with his will, will receive many lashes, but the one who did not know it, and committed deeds worthy of a flogging, will receive but few. *From everyone who has been given much, much will be required; and to whom they entrusted much, of him they will ask all the more" (Luke 12: 47-48)*. It is true that He does not require the same from all of us, but nonetheless He *does* deserve and desire to have *all* of us—no matter how little we think we have to offer. He adopted us into His family, and we are heirs of God and fellow heirs with Christ (Roman 8:15-17). We all have different personalities, different gifts, and different adjectives to describe Him; that's the beauty of the Body.

"Ask, and it will be given to you; seek, and you shall find; knock, and it shall be opened to you. For everyone who asks receives, and he who seeks finds, and to him who knocks it shall be open" (Matthew 7:7-8). Does that mean we can have whatever we want? **No.** If we come before Him with a broken spirit, though, He will lead us through the desert, showing us things we never saw before. Sacrificing to Him will become our greatest joy instead of our greatest fear. We may lose our friends, our health, our status, our very life, but isn't that what dying to self is all about? The benefits *far* outweigh any losses.

May God continue to refine each of us, putting us through the fire for our own good.

APRIL 13-14, 2005-NO MATTER WHAT

My heart is heavy tonight, and I can't really articulate why. I guess, in a way, I feel like I've had the wind knocked out of me this week and I'm still recovering from the initial blow. I *do* trust, and I *will* follow—no matter what. At the same time, I am feeling very human and very small.

There are so many things I want to accomplish in my life, and a lot of those can't be done from my bedroom. At the same time, there are *so* many ministry opportunities He's given me right here. His will may not always make sense to my finite mind, but I am learning ever so slowly that His ways are *always* best.

After several months of this, I'm physically exhausted. But it goes deeper than that. Some days my mind feels like even it's slowing down. Every day is a battle on so many fronts. I cannot let Satan have a foothold, though; he'll take a mile if I let him. I will press on for the higher calling, no matter where that leads me. They can put chest tubes in me, put me on a respirator, and even use the saw if they want. *Nothing* is going to shake my confidence in Him. He will get the glory that He so rightfully deserves, even if that means I have to wait much longer than I would like to get the ball rolling. It's *not* about me, after all. "Jesus Christ **is** the same yesterday and today and forever" (Hebrews 13:8 NIV).

20 MINUTES LATER...

I don't know what has happened to me, but I asked God to meet me where I was, and He did in a big way. I was feeling absolutely emotionally depleted, and I was just going to hit the hay. But God had bigger plans.

First of all, I opened my Bible—good plan. Romans 15:5-7 says, "Now may the God who gives perseverance and encouragement grant you to be of the same mind with one another according to Christ Jesus, so that with one accord you may with one voice glorify the God and Father of our Lord Jesus Christ. Therefore, accept one another, just as Christ also accepted us to the glory of God."

All I want to do is glorify God. That is my passion and heartbeat, the reason I wake up in the morning. Nothing on this earth could keep me here, but it makes it worthwhile knowing that just living and breathing brings Him glory. I feel so at peace again, and it's a wonderful feeling! I have felt so frustrated, but now my heart feels free again! The chains have once again been broken. Hallelujah!

The Father is meeting me here tonight, and I feel so unworthy. My frustration may not have been wrong, but it was a really weird feeling for me. I'm so used to feeling close to the Father, and I hated the way I felt. I felt so—trapped. It's hard to explain, I guess.

All I know is this: *I love You, Father! I will serve You. I will die for You, but it is my highest honor to live for You, to give You every breath and every moment. It is well with my soul, Lord. Take all of me, the little I have, and make me what You want me to be. Kill me if You have to. I do not hold on to anything in my life, no matter how significant. Father, I pray You will continue to show me exactly what You want me to do. May Satan not get a foothold in my life, causing me discouragement and frustration and taking my eyes off You. I want my gaze to be fully on You, my Healer, Redeemer, and coming King. Every part of me that does not align with Your will is like filthy rags; make me fully clean and fully Yours. Soli Deo Gloria.*

When peace, like a river, attendeth
my way, When sorrows like sea billows roll;
Whatever my lot, Thou has taught me to say,
"It is well, it is well with my soul"
My sin—O the bliss
of this glorious thought,
My sin—not in part, but the whole,

Is nailed to the cross
And I bear it no more,
Praise the Lord,
Praise the Lord, O my soul!
And, Lord, haste the day
when my faith shall be sight,
The clouds be rolled back as a scroll:
The trump shall resound
and the Lord shall descend,
"Even so"—it is well with my soul. —AMEN[9]

APRIL 21, 2005-BEAUTY FROM PAIN

I looked in the mirror today, and I didn't recognize myself.
I don't look in the mirror much; I don't have a reason to do so.
I don't do my hair or put my contacts in. I wash my face and
brush my teeth, but I don't stop to glance in the mirror. Every
day is the exact same—me with my glasses on and my hair pulled
up (occasionally in a pencil).

I got back some pictures from a wedding I attended and,
I'll admit, they made me smile. I recognized that girl, all dressed
up with her hair curled. I may have been dead tired the day they
were taken, but I didn't care. I'm *not* saying that I'm focusing
on how I look physically or that I think I'm the most attractive
woman to grace the face of the earth—not at all. I *do*, though,
think about it now and then. I'm a woman, after all.

My blue eyes look so tired. Even though spiritually I feel so
alive, it isn't obvious from looking at me. I still laugh and smile
all the time, yet sometimes it makes me so tired to do so. When
I say, "I can't breathe," when I'm laughing with someone on the
phone, I'm being serious. It's funny, yet it's really not. I can't
wait until I can laugh without coughing. I don't even remember
how that feels!

I know that God has been guiding *every single* one of my steps
thus far, and He promises never to leave my side as we continue

on. I can't help but feel overwhelmed, though. It's all so beautiful, yet so scary. I cannot think of any other way to describe it but "breathtaking."

The Lord knows my heart is heavy right now for so many reasons, but I choose to love life and love the One who made me *free*. The Cross means so much more to me now, and I know once I wake up from my surgery it will mean even more. I am getting a second chance at life, a chance that I certainly do not deserve.

I am looking forward to my twentieth birthday. I want to have 200 candles instead of twenty. I couldn't even blow out six at my nineteenth birthday party, so I think we'll all cry if I actually blow out 200. So I'll get the color back in my face and my eyes will be bright once more. Until then, I will *not* allow the fire burning within my heart to go out. I will press on, knowing that the refining taking place is for my own good. I love You, Father, with all that I have and all I will ever be. After all this has passed, I will fall flat on my face and praise You for all You are. Until then, I will physically get on my face as much as I can.

Lord, I can't wait until I can sing at the top of my lungs to You, laugh for You, dance for You, and breathe every breath for You and You alone. After I've cried my last, there truly will be beauty from pain.

APRIL 23, 2005–WEARY

"Man is like a mere breath; His days are like a passing shadow."

—Psalm 144:4

As today wore on, I continued to be in a good mood, waiting anxiously for my phone call. I ate lunch, answered a few calls from friends, took a shower, and waited some more... and some more. The call never came. I'm *still* not listed, as of 12:41 this morning.

After four months of being home from Cedarville University, I am still not listed on the U.N.O.S. That frustrates me. I'm not going to flat-out lie and say that every fiber within me is absolutely thrilled that, for like the eighth time, I'm not listed! I am so ready to get this part of it all over with. Being listed is half the battle. I know I have a long road ahead of me, but I can't exactly have the surgery if I am not listed! I will hold tightly to His promise: He will never leave me nor forsake me. Even if I don't get listed until the end of May, He'd still be in complete control. He knew before I was even born what day I was going to be listed and what day I would have my surgery. Nothing I do can trump God's omniscience. He hasn't and never will forget about me. He has this under control. Further along, I'll truly understand why. Lord willing, it will be tomorrow.

So once more, I dealt with the whole thing of not being listed. I guess it really wasn't *that* much of a surprise. The longer I go without being listed, the harder it is to even picture myself getting better. I know that sounds silly, but it's true. I know in my heart that, Lord willing, I'm going to sing and dance again, but that's a whole other world away from me now. I have a *long* road ahead of me. Yes, it frustrates me, but I continue to give that over to the Lord every day.

I know it's not wrong to want to get better, but part of me feels selfish even thinking about it. It is such an honor and privilege to carry my cross, and my cross right now is being sick and looking the part. I am human, though, and it's only normal to want to be able to breathe again and dance in the moonlight.

I am feeling better now. I feel silly sitting here with tears streaming down my face, but I feel beautiful. I just wish Jesus were physically here with me so He could hold my hand and look me in the eye and tell me how much He truly does love me. I will stay here, though, and serve Him while I can. He loves me and He has called me. He's *captivated* by my smile, and even though I'm so very tired right now, He doesn't love me any less.

So dancing or no dancing, breathing or no breathing, I smile up at heaven and I am happy.

APRIL 23, 2005-SURRENDER

"As for me, I know that my Redeemer lives, And at the last He will take His stand on the earth. Even after my skin is destroyed, yet from my flesh I shall see God."

—Job 19:26-27

Recently I have become more and more aware of just how irreplaceable I am on this journey. What I mean to say is that God has given me such a blessing, allowing me to minister to many, many people. No one else can bring glory to Him in the same manner I can, more importantly, as any of us can. We all can be swept up into our irreplaceable roles if we just allow Him to put us where He may. That may be China, a bedroom, or a college 3,000 miles from the nearest family member or friend. No matter where we go, though, we will not be going alone. He is always there, no matter what time of day. We may not even feel like we're doing anything for the kingdom once we get there, but rest-assured, if we're where He wants us, we are. People we don't even know are counting on us to take up our cross and follow hard after Him, no matter how we feel about it.

Loving God is a choice every single day. God works in mysterious ways, if we only allow Him to have full reign in our lives. He can continue to use us, even if we feel like we aren't where we could be, spiritually. Satan will try to get us to buy into the lie that God cannot use us if we are feeling any hint of frustration, stress, or any other human emotion. That is just not the case. We are humans, and certainly working for the kingdom is not based on emotion; it's based on a commitment to Jesus Christ. We should not be afraid to experience emotions that come with being one of His creations; He wired us with emotions and feelings for a reason. As long as we are not ruled by the emotions we may feel throughout a given day, God can still use us.

God is always around. I talk to Him all the time, telling Him how much I love Him and want to be His and His alone. He makes me smile, and He always responds, too. The secret? Read His Word. Pray. Look out the window at creation. Hug someone. Look someone in the eye. Laugh. Being able to do those things is a gift from the Lord in and of itself. I love the simple things. I don't need much; all I need is Him. He's all I'll ever need and more. He loves me just the way I am, too! He's my best friend, the King of my heart and my greatest Joy. In life or death, I know my Redeemer lives.

APRIL 27, 2005
Finally listed on the U.N.O.S.
at 3:30 in the afternoon

APRIL 27, 2005–DAY #1: IT HAS FINALLY COME

Day #1 on the list is officially over!

I am indeed listed! I keep saying it over and over to myself in disbelief. For so many months I have been waiting for this day, and it's finally here. In a way it feels like I'm engaged. Getting on the list is like getting engaged, and having the actual surgery will be like getting married! I hope my groom (the lungs) waits at least a week to come for me, or I will be one stressed-out bride. I always say I won't care if my future fiancé gives me a bread tie, but in this deal I get something better than a diamond! He

(Jesus) is taking my breath away and then giving it back to me tenfold.

I called so many people this afternoon that it was quite comical. Columbus called at 3:30 on the dot, and by 3:40, I think I had already called four people. Reactions ran the whole gamut—from crying to screaming in excitement. I don't know where the burst of energy I got came from. So many emailed and instant messaged me with their phone numbers and encouragement!

Although I am extremely excited, I am *well* aware that the road ahead will be long and hard. This has not and will not be easy once I have my surgery. Things are bound to get more complicated, at least in the beginning. I am *so* thankful, though, that He is in control. Yes, I want everyone to be home when I go into surgery, but if they aren't, they aren't. I can't do a thing about it. I love them all so much, but I still must go through those double doors alone. So no matter if they're 1,000 miles away or just in the next room, I know it will be God's will and He is still worthy. I also know that I'm not going to come out of surgery and be asking immediately for my cell phone and some strawberries. The first couple of days, especially, will be rough, probably much worse than I can even imagine. I have felt like a train wreck before, but I doubt that compares to what I'm about to go through. I'm game for anything, though—I think. So, tonight I go to sleep with my phone near me, knowing it could go off at any minute. I will thank my Father for His never-ending love, freedom, and patience. Lord, let it be less of me and more of You. It's truly *not* about me.

FALSE ALARM #1

May 5, 2005

- Called by Columbus Children's at 8:30 A.M. and told to get down to Columbus <u>ASAP</u>—a possible donor was supposedly available
- Had been listed for transplant for only eight days at the time and told it would most likely be at least two months until I got called, if not longer

The email frantically written at 9:00 A.M....
May 5, 2005 (THIS IS IT, LORD-WILLING)

THEY CALLED

At 8:45 A.M. Columbus called to inform me that a donor had become available. I know you're asking why in the world am I on here, but I don't have to leave until 11:00 A.M., so I had to get this email out! I'm doing pretty well with it all. I've cried a few tears, made a few phone calls, and I'm not shaking as badly as I was an hour ago. God is so good! I was praying this wouldn't happen for another forty-eight hours, but if this is what He wants, then I will serve Him with a willing heart.

This may be a false alarm. If so, I'll be back with more tonight. If not, I love you guys, and I am so very thankful for your encouragement and support! Please be in prayer as I go into surgery (Lord-willing)!!! I'll be home to you all in three to four weeks.

May we keep our eyes on Jesus, the author and finisher of our faith. ONLY He is worthy of ALL our praise! To Him be the honor, the glory, and the praise FOREVER! I will serve my King in life or death and, starting now, that phrase means so much more..

All my love,
Amber Nicole Metz

MAY 5, 2005-DRESS REHEARSAL

WOW—WHAT A DAY…

Well, today was indeed a false alarm. I will be going back and redoing this all again some day. I know people were praying and were excited and scared at the same time. Keep praying, though. My day is coming!

I'm at a complete loss for words and extremely tired. I just wanted to let everyone know that I'm home and doing well (as well as I can be, that is). God is in control and, although I may not always understand His ways, I am so glad it's He who's running the show instead of me!

He has given me one of the most experienced transplant teams in the world, and I do not take that for granted. Dr. Astor knows what he's doing, and I trust his judgment completely. I have the utmost respect for that man; he just turned down his first pair of lungs here in Ohio. I'm sure he's looking forward to having one transplant here in the Buckeye state under his belt, and Lord willing, it's not far off. He says organ procurement is definitely more of an art than a science. There's so much more to it than just a bunch of numbers and measurements. After all, ultimately, my life is in the Lord's hands, and He's the greatest physician ever. Dr. Astor could have just gone ahead with the surgery and taken some chances, but he's choosing to be patient and wait for better. In his words, "only the best for Amber." I like his way of thinking!

For now, I leave you. Today was indeed a dress rehearsal, but we cannot view life that way. Each day counts for the Kingdom, and we don't get any do-overs. Tomorrow could be our last day; who are we to say otherwise? We are to live every day for the One who created us, and rest peacefully in His arms. He'll see us through.

I can't explain the peace I had today, except to say it was totally from God! I am so very thankful for all the prayers coming from all directions! I had people praying all around the country, and I know they'll do it again when the time comes back around. I am so thankful that the Lord is allowing me to be a witness in so many different ways. My demeanor comes from Him and Him alone. I'm sure Dr. Astor was glad I didn't get upset when he came in to tell me that we weren't going to do it. God completely moved in amazing ways, and I'm sure the recipient of the right lung was tremendously blessed (they didn't end up using the left one). Organ donation is such a beautiful thing, and I am very thankful that there are people out there who are willing to be a part of it.

As soon as I knew I could go home, I sent my dad after a Mountain Dew, threw off all the monitors, grabbed my stuff, and hightailed it out the door. I was just praying they weren't going to call me back today. I seriously need a few days to recover from all this, emotionally and physically.

Driving home in the beautiful weather, I couldn't help but be happy to be alive. The sun was shining down on me in the car, my music was blasting in my headphones, and I was at peace with my life. I was safe. I was alive. I was once again learning to *completely* trust my Heavenly Father.

So I'm staying right where I am. He's leading the way just fine. I don't need to run ahead and check it out just to make sure. No, He won't lead me astray. I'm here to say I love Him, and I will serve Him until my dying day. I guess tonight everything just kind of hit me. I really could have had my surgery; I was that close but yet so far. I have to be ready to go at any time, ready to have an answer for the hope that is within me because I know I could not do this on my own! I am a failure and a fraud without Christ, but He within me gives me power and courage to press on. This journey is not about Amber Metz! I know Christ is working in so many more lives than just mine, and I pray I am being the vessel He wants me to be. He could have picked anyone else, and many times I wonder why He did indeed choose me, but I do not take the calling lightly. It is a blessing and a privilege to walk the path He has laid in front of me.

MOTHER'S DAY

MAY 8, 2005-MOTHER'S DAY
MOTHER'S DAY..

Since it *is* Mother's Day, I thought it would be fitting to dote on my own mom a little. She and I may be like night and day in personality, but she's still my mom. I am blown away by her strength and ability to do a million things in twenty-four hours time. I fail *so* often to stop and think about just how much my mom has done for me and continues to do without complaining. I pray that when I (Lord willing) have a household of my own, I will exude *many* of the traits my mom shows around the Metz household every single day. Most women have not been put in the position my mom is in, and her attitude about it all makes me very proud to call her *my* mom.

I've been home for five months now, and there have definitely been days I could barely do anything for myself. My mom's not a very vocal person, but she's told me many times that her unspeakable joy will be when I can get out of my room and be able to enjoy my life again. I do enjoy my life now, but I know what she means. It has to be extremely difficult for her, as a mother, to watch me in the state I'm in.

It wasn't always like this, though. Of course I wasn't well before, but I certainly wasn't as sick as I am now. It was so nice to get away for a while and go to Cedarville for a semester, and even though I swore I'd never come back, I'm here. God certainly had different plans for me. I had my freedom and independence for a while and, Lord willing, I am about to have it again. The lessons I have learned, though, will stay with me forever and have an impact on my life and ministry for the rest of my life.

I've learned a lot about my mom since I came home again after being gone for four months. Yes, we're completely different people, that is obvious, but I don't focus so much on the differences anymore. God made her the way she is for a reason, and God made me the way I am for a reason. It's as simple as that. I don't have to be her, and she doesn't have to be me. The important thing is that we are both striving to be the women God wants us to be, women after His own heart. Our personalities sometimes clash, but I think she and I both have come to respect our differences, and we're learning to embrace what we do have in common. I love my mom very much, and I was happy that today I wasn't in ICU but instead here with my mom in our own home, giving her Mother's Day gift to her. Friends may come and go, our lives may change drastically, but we never would have even had life to begin with without our mothers. Father, may we never forget…

MAY 9, 2005-WALKING WITH GOD
DAY # 12 ON THE LIST IS OVER!

Oh how I long to see His will accomplished in my life. I know that there's no secret solution to finding the will of God. We aren't going to find it in some book on prayer or in some twelve-step program.

You want the will of God for your life?

Then hold fast to Micah 6:8: "He has told you, O man, what is good; And what does the LORD require of you but to do justice, to love kindness, and to walk humbly with your God?"

The past twenty-four hours have definitely been a time of "Lord, I believe. Please just help my unbelief." Questions like, "What if none of this is even *real?*" played like a tape in my mind. I was honestly sick and tired of being sick and tired. I wanted to have some control for once. As Christians, we're called to *daily* die to ourselves, but *why* is the question. Is it so the 'Big Guy' upstairs is happy and will give us a bigger mansion, or is it so our pious life will make our peers feel bad and then they'll get their act together and follow suit?

It all comes back to motive. *Why* do we serve God? We may be doing all the right things, but if our motives are not pure, it doesn't mean a *thing*. If we've been living off our "fire insurance," and we attend Sunday school, Sunday worship service, and Wednesday night service just so we can make sure God knew we were at church serving Him, well, then there's a *big* problem. That's not serving God at all. What happened to all the other moments in your life? Christ calls us to love the Lord our God with *all* our heart, mind, and soul. I think that means *all* the time, not just when the doors of the church are open. Yes, salvation is free to *us*, but it certainly wasn't free to Christ.

Maybe we serve on every committee in our church, pray for every missionary known to man, and hold a Bible study in our home. People with that kind of résumé look like they'd be quite effective Christians, but if they're only doing it so they'd be noticed in the church, then they're doing a disservice to the body of Christ. Serving the Lord is not a nine-to-five job. He doesn't want to find out how appreciated our dedication to the Lord is from Peter, Paul, and Mary's prayers, when we haven't prayed *ourselves* in days, weeks, or even months.

May we not forget that people *are* watching us. We may never know how we've influenced, positively or negatively, the people we come in contact with every single day. *We are to always* be ready to have an answer for the hope that is within us, and not be surprised if opportunities to do so show up out of the blue.

Today has been very long, but I am going to bed with the assurance that God will be watching over me while I sleep and be waiting to spend time with me when I wake up. God is **always** willing to spend time with His children, if we will just meet Him in the stillness and allow Him to hold our hearts in His hands. I have come to appreciate the hours I have every day to spend with my Savior. I'm really not sure how I'm going to adjust to when (Lord willing) I no longer have to sit in my room all the time.

MAY 17, 2005-JESUS IN THE GARDEN DAY #20 ON THE LIST IS OVER!

I am in awe of who God is not only in my life, but in the lives of the ones I love as well. He has proven Himself to be so very faithful time and time again. Even when the bottom falls out, He is there to catch us. He dries our tears, loves our laugh, and longs for us to speak His name. There truly is nothing else needed in this life but Him. So many times in the past couple of days, I have longed to be able to understand what is happening around me, but I have been reminded in so many ways tonight of this verse: "Be still and know that I am God; I will be exalted among the nations, I will be exalted in the earth" (Psalm 46:10 NIV).

I'm *not* God. I've learned how to give over the reins of my life to God, allowing Him to work in me however He may. But I'm getting a crash course right now in giving over control when it comes to the ones I love. I knew it was coming. I just had this feeling that God's whole "Do you trust me, Amber?" question was an ongoing thing, involving many different facets of my life.

Tonight I thought about when Jesus was praying in the garden before the guards seized him and took Him away to be crucified. He was praying to His heavenly Father asking if the cup might pass from Him. He had known for so long that He was appointed to die and become the sacrificial lamb for all of mankind, but that did not stop Him from asking if it would be possible to go about redemption some other way. In the end, though, He finished His powerful prayer with "not My will, but Yours be done."

It is remarkable and encouraging to see that even Jesus was brutally honest when He prayed. He didn't say, "Well, God, bring on the guards! This is going to be a blast! Man, I'm glad we got a good meal in before I bite the dust." He was more than prepared to do the job at hand. But at the same time, He was obviously grieved. He was human, after all. I think it's that He even took time to pray, considering He was God. If Jesus prayed and He is the Son of God, think how much we should be praying! Prayer seems pretty crucial to me.

Obviously, since Jesus was without sin, opening up to God and telling Him how He really felt is not a sin. Am I praying to gripe and complain to God about how I didn't get my way, or am I truly longing for Him to reveal Himself to me and make my path straight? May I always long for the Lord's will and not my own.

I do trust Him, and I will rest in His assurance that He is in complete control. Some moments I long to be out of this flesh and up in heaven. I want to hear "well done," not for my own gain, but because Jesus really is proud of me and the woman I've become. I just want to bring His name honor and glory in all I do, and I long to see others take hold of His freedom.

I'm trying so very hard down here, Father. I just feel so broken right now, and I know I need to rely solely on You...I love You and will serve You for as long as You allow me to draw breath. Why does it have to be so hard, though? I guess we weren't meant to understand; but I will continue to walk by faith.

MAY 26, 2005-JOURNEY IN PROGRESS
DAY #29 ON THE LIST IS OVER!

Another day is over, and I find myself feeling as though I'm in somewhat of a fog. So much has been happening around me recently that I honestly have been forgetting that I'm going into major surgery soon. After a conversation tonight on the phone, I was brought back to reality and now things are fresh in my mind again. It's really happening, and soon. How soon? Only God knows that and honestly only He should be privy to that information.

It's not so much about me as it is about all of the ones who want to be here. I want that for them. Then again, is it really that big a deal if they're there or here or somewhere else? God is God. He hears the prayers of His children whether they're at the bottom of the ocean or somewhere in outer space. He's not bound by a couple of hundred or even a thousand miles. I know if the time comes when my friends will all have to leave and I haven't had my surgery yet, I'll put on a very brave face and tell them all I'll see them when they get home. I'll reassure them that God's in control and that everything will happen in His timing, whether or not they're gone.

I'm glad that God doesn't try to teach me everything at once. He knows what I can handle and what I can't, and I'm learning more and more that being a disciple of Jesus requires me to put on my sandals and set out on a journey, following Him wherever He may lead. I shouldn't pack a list of objectives for Jesus, either. He doesn't need my agendas. All He needs is my heart; He'll take care of the rest. I cannot worship the journey, but I must embrace the path that God has set before me and desire Him and Him alone along the long, dusty road.

If some of the events in my life that have taken place recently had occurred a year or two ago, I probably would have thrown up my hands by now. It has certainly been a whirlwind of activity. But I'm *so* very thankful for His love and constant support! God truly does know what He's doing. At the end of the day, I fall asleep in His arms, knowing that no one will ever love me the way He does.

MAY 28, 2005

...a year after graduation

MAY 28, 2005-OBEYING
DAY #31 ON THE LIST IS OVER!

"...Farewell the neighing steed and the shrill trump,
The spirit-stirring drum, the ear-piercing fife,
The royal banner, and all quality,
Pride, pomp, and circumstance of glorious war!"
—*Pomp & Circumstance* by Elgar[10]

Complete surrender is a matter of leaning back and allowing myself to fall into His arms, knowing that if He doesn't catch me, I'll crash and burn. It's more than just eternity at stake, though; there's so much more. Freedom and true happiness will only be found in Christ and Christ alone. The only reason I have the choice to choose Him is because of Him. So, in a sense, He chose me from the very beginning! The God of the universe knows my name and can offer me Eternal freedom that starts now through His Son, Jesus Christ!

In any case, I am in awe of my Heavenly Father and His perfect timing. Time and time again He proves to me that any plans that I could ever come up with pale in comparison to His perfect will. I don't know why in the world I'd even want to think about going off on my own and trying to manage my way through this thing we call life. It has to be a rough road out there without a compass, a constant companion to turn to, and a hope that goes beyond this world. I cannot rely on mere humans to get me through. I may live a very successful, envied life by earthly standards, but one day this world is going to pass away and the Son will be the sun and only things done with eternity in mind will remain.

I find myself longing for that day when I'll be in my glorified body and worshiping Jesus at His feet instead of feeling as though I'm talking to the air. I long to see every knee bow and every tongue confess that Jesus Christ is Lord of all, for Him to get the glory He so rightfully deserves, and for all the wrongs to be made right. I'm not there yet, though, and I am more than content with where He has me now. At the same time, I am not content with staying exactly where I am now in my spiritual life. I want to draw closer to my heavenly Father and lay aside everything in my path that hinders me from doing so. Jesus is the way, the truth, and the life, and the only way to the Father. Nothing I will ever say can save anyone; only the Holy Spirit can move in each heart.

It's funny how time changes everything. A year ago I was in my cap and gown graduating and running around like a mad woman the entire day. Today it's almost 5:00 P.M., and I'm in my pjs, hardly doing a thing, just waiting for a new pair of lungs, dreaming about what it'll be like when I'll be able to run all over creation again, doing a million things at once. What a day that will be!

The last year has brought so many changes, and I feel like a completely different person in so many ways. There's one thing I do know for sure, though: I would not trade the journey for anything.

MAY 30, 2005–AMAZING DAY #33 ON THE LIST IS OVER!

I'm learning to be thankful for even the smallest things: smiles from strangers, little girls who want to know why I have oxygen, people who get on my nerves (yes, even them)—the list could go on. On Friday I had one of the most hilarious yet humbling experiences of my life. I went to Columbus for a check-up, and I had to meet with the marketing team. They're doing a documentary on me since I'll most likely be the first person to receive a double lung transplant at Columbus Children's.

The first plan was to take pictures and video. But then it was becoming too hard to fit everything into my schedule, so we just took some pictures and then I headed off to get an echocardiogram/EKG. I was told we'd just do the video part at a later date. But all that changed at the last minute. Tama, the director of marketing, came and found me after I was done with all my testing and asked if we could get some video of my friend Lindsey and me walking through the hospital and then of her interviewing me outside. Even though I was extremely tired and hungry (I hadn't eaten since the night before), I agreed to the filming and put my best face forward, knowing that if I got it done and out of the way, I wouldn't have to worry about it later. So Lindsey and I grabbed my stuff and headed out with a cameraman following us along the way.

I had gone to Columbus that day thinking that if they did a video it would be me in the video, not me and Lindsey. I was dressed for the occasion, while Lindsey was not. She and I couldn't stop laughing, because here I was in a white dress suit, while she was in jeans and a T-shirt. So Lindsey and I were supposed to act as though Bill, the cameraman, wasn't there and just go about our business. That was easier said than done, because at one point Bill was practically on the ground in front of us filming our feet as we walked. It was odd. When Lindsey and I get together, we can laugh at about anything, so you can imagine how hard it was for us to keep a straight face.

We finally made it to the front of the hospital, and Tama decided we'd go outside and hold a mini-interview on a bench. It was an absolutely gorgeous day, so I was more than happy to get some fresh air. First they filmed Lindsey and me talking outside and acting like we were reading the books we had with us. After that, Tama started our interview. I don't remember exactly what all she asked me, but I do remember that anything she said, I brought it straight back to my faith and what God has been doing in my life. I pray that I don't say that out of pride, but I don't know what else to talk about other than the freedom that I have found in Christ. My relationship with Jesus Christ permeates every facet of my life, and I have absolutely nothing without Him.

I do remember that Tama asked me what I thought of the concept of organ donation and what brought me to Columbus, etc. The interview was probably ten minutes. She finished asking all of her questions, and when I looked up, the cameraman looked like he could cry. Tama was just staring at me as if she was in shock. After she got her composure, Tama proceeded to tell me how I should be in Congress and showered me with other compliments. The cameraman told me he'd done hundreds of these interviews and that no one ever talked about their faith as I had. He said he could tell my faith was obviously very important to me and offered me a lot of hope. He said he meets a lot of confident people but he could still feel that sense of desperation, but with me, he said that he could tell I was way above that. I didn't even know what to say except that my strength comes from Christ and Christ alone. I had the privilege to once again bring the glory back to Him and to Him alone.

My head was spinning after all that, and the best part hadn't even happened yet! As I was getting ready to walk back into the hospital to finally go home, this lady stopped us. She went up to

Tama and asked her when my story would be on TV. Tama really didn't have an answer for her, because as we all know, no one knows when things are going to happen. I honestly didn't think much about this woman coming up to us, considering there was a video camera out in front of the hospital focused on a girl with oxygen. The world is filled with nosy people. I just figured she wanted to know what was going on. I quickly realized, though, that this was not the case–at all. The woman said to me, "I was sitting here listening to you the whole time (I still don't know how she heard me) and I have never seen such joy and hope in someone. I have never felt so much contentment listening to someone before. You spoke to me, and this God you speak of is using you to touch others' lives. It's obvious that you have something special, and God loves you."

When she was finished I just stood there in complete and utter shock. There was so much racing around in my head, but I couldn't even seem to get any words out. I was finally able to say, "God loves you too, Ma'am," and then I asked her if I could give her a hug. I didn't know what else to do. Part of me wanted to bust out with the Gospel right then and there, but I just felt led to hold the lady close and be Jesus to her in that way. I wiped away tears as I walked away. I get chills every time I think about it, even two days after the fact.

It was obvious that the Holy Spirit moved across that courtyard, and although I will probably never see that woman again, I do know that seeds were planted. I am thankful that God gave me the opportunity to be Jesus to a mystery woman at the hospital even though I was tired, hungry, and so ready to eat!

JUNE 2005

- Had been home from Cedarville University for six months
- Had experienced a false alarm a month before
- FEV1 remained stable, yet I was getting weaker by the month
- Oxygen therapy remained ongoing and slightly increased
- Friends returned home from college for summer vacation
- Thought of transplant occurring during the summer seemed like a certainty to all of us

Reflections

Stacy:

Amber..

My quick wit always made you laugh till you couldn't breathe through the pain

The fear that gripped my heart in those moments I can't explain,

Feeling helpless as I watched weakness invade.

Once the state lines separated us, my faith began to fade;

Prayer my only ally, as I listened through the miles.

You gave your all to Jesus, still feeling inadequate but with a smile.

Nothing kept you down, or dampened your determination

To be an ambassador of the gospel, a living testimony of salvation.

Anticipation and waiting, the period of agonizing suspense

Seemed only to fuel your passion for Him, without the slightest pretense.

The night your miracle came was a night forever engraved in my mind,

Waiting with bated breath, my cell phone handy at my side

The hours rolled past, hardly noticed, as I listened for new tips.

"She's out of surgery," they said, a sigh of relief escaped my lips.

This will just be the beginning, a long road to recovery yet to face.

You battled it most valiantly, being ever the uncommon case,

A phenomenal recovery; a testimony of His power in your life.

Blessings to His name for you were healed beyond our dreams

Empowered now to tell the world of all He's done, your face it gleams

Just like Moses on Mount Sinai, God's truths written on your heart.

His blessings will continue as you seek His truth to impart.

I thank Him daily that I've known you and seen firsthand His grace,

We'll continue to make memories no one will ever erase.

Now that you can laugh without fear of losing all your air

The world around us better watch out for this dynamic pair!

From: Stacy Anderson

Location: Toccoa Falls, Georgia

Relationship: One of Amber's best friends, met through the TFC ministry team.

JUNE 1, 2005–FOLLOW THE SON
DAY # 35 ON THE LIST IS OVER!

If God knows the depths of my heart, then He already knows that I've been struggling the past few days. There are a lot of things going on right now, and I am constantly being brought to my knees, where I belong. I'm not doubting my faith or wishing that my life were different, not at all. I feel very humbled by the position I am in, and I wouldn't trade my life for health, wealth, love, or anything else for that matter. No amount of money or any person on this earth could ever make me feel as secure as I do when I'm in sweet communion with my heavenly Father. At the same time, though, I long for transparency with human beings, for the ability to say what I really want to say without fear. I long for the ability to protect my loved ones from dangers that lie ahead and, most of all, for the ability to let go of them and allow them to learn, knowing that the same God who has led me through the valley so many times is right by their side too. He's not going anywhere, and as long as they keep their gaze fixed on Him, His will will be accomplished.

I am only responsible for myself—a lesson I've learned time and time again over the course of the past year. For the first time, though, this lesson is hitting really close to home. I do not need transparency with a human to survive, though. God is always available to talk to, and numerous others surround me, as well. So why does my heart hurt so much?

Lindsey, Joni, and I made our way out to the country tonight and watched the sunset in a farmer's field. It was one of the most beautiful sights I've ever seen, and the whole time I was thinking about the beauty of my Lord and His gift of freedom to me through His Son, Jesus Christ. I kept telling Joni to "follow the sun" when we were driving out to find a spot, but now I see that I was talking to myself.

Follow the Son, Amber. You don't need anyone but Him. Love can only reach so far until I have to let go and go forward in faith, knowing that I'll be there with open arms, day or night, when they come back around. For the time being, I will hold on to His promise that He'll never leave me or forsake me. He knows me, all of me, and He loves me still. Why, I don't know. I'm *so* glad God doesn't give us all the answers.

Oh, Father, please dry my tears and wrap Your arms around me tonight while I sleep. I love You with all that I have, and I long for others to live for the cause of Christ, as well. It certainly beats anything this world has to offer... I've laid down so very much, and I wouldn't trade any of it for the world. Thank You for wanting my whole heart and for taking each piece that I gave until You had the whole thing. You have it all now, Lord. Oh how I love, Father, but my love can only go so far. Because I love, I pray for Your will. Do what You may. I love You.

JUNE 2, 2005–STEADY ON
DAY #36 ON THE LIST IS OVER!

I'm so thankful that the Lord knows what's on my heart, because the words just haven't been coming together lately. I am thankful for the little things, though, such as sunsets in the country (two nights in a row) and apple juice in sippy cups. Yes, I was regressing into my childhood when everything was so much simpler.

Part of me wishes that I was three years old again with the blonde curls and not a care in the world. Nothing could harm me, or so I thought, and the sky was the limit when it came to my dreams. I worshipped the ground my parents walked on, and I thought the world was in love with me. I was so innocent— such a free spirit and a riot.

Times have changed. I'm no longer that three-year-old. God was watching over me sixteen years ago when I was three, and He's still watching over me now! I don't need anyone else or anything else but Him. I desperately long to do His will, and I know that as long as I keep on walking, He'll lead me through whatever valley I come up against. I just have to remember that His timing isn't always my timing, nor should it be. His ways are always higher than mine, sweeter than mine, and so much more fulfilling than anything my finite mind could ever come up with. He loves me and He knows my heart. That's all that matters. Words aren't always needed, and sometimes they just seem to get in the way.

So I'm going to continue to follow Him into the unknown. I have no idea what I'm doing about school, or even when (or if) I'll get better, or where the Lord will lead me. But despite all that I do not know, I do know this: I love Him, and I know He loves me more than I will ever understand. He has called me. He's preparing the way to accomplish His will in my life. I couldn't be more honored than to be on this journey with Him in the driver's seat. Yes, I get tired and restless, but that doesn't change the burning passion within me to love Him with all that I am and to shine His light into the darkest places. My heart is crying "forward" yet "stoppp!" all at the same time. I can't stop, though. I must keep trusting in the promise of knowing that whatever happens, He was always in control from the beginning.

JUNE 4, 2005–HIS DAY #38 ON THE LIST IS OVER!

I am floored by Jesus' sacrifice that bought me my freedom, but I know my understanding of just how much I've been blessed is about the same as an infant's understanding of Calculus II. One day, though, I will see Jesus face-to-face and my faith will be made sight. I cannot wait for that day! I just wish I could love Him the way He so rightfully deserves. At the same time, all He's ever asked for is all of me. I may not be much, but He can surely have everything I have to offer. When we give Him the canvas of our lives, He can make a gorgeous picture out of what seems like just old, dusty paper.

I know I'm not always the brightest crayon in the box, the most sensible, or a good practitioner of moderation at times. I do know, though, that despite my flaws, God wants to use me, to break me for my own good, and to love me as only He ever could. He just wants me to talk to Him when I'm scared, thank Him when I'm laughing, and take Him with me wherever I go. Most of all, He wants me to be me, and right now I'm exhausted, anxious, and feeling oh so very human. At the same time, I feel alive and willing to get out there and testify to what the Lord has done in my life, if I only had the energy to do so.

Lord willing, one day very soon I will be the proud owner of a new set of lungs. The day is coming; I can feel it. I'm going to get well. When I do I won't look back. I cannot wait to get out and proclaim His name. Once I'm well, I'm not going to go off the deep end and completely forsake everything I've learned and who I've become. Lord, strike me dead if I do! May I never take for granted what I've been through all the nights I didn't have anyone to turn to but the Lord and all the little miracles I've seen along the way. I have a long way to go, I know that, but He's brought me this far. I'm sure He'll continue to lead me through this valley that, at times, seems to have no end. In His name, I press on.

JUNE 5, 2005–A CHOICE
DAY #39 ON THE LIST IS OVER!

This week has been nothing short of extremely trying for me. I've been exhausted in more ways than one. Waves of frustration, anxiety, and guilt have come without end. Spiritually speaking, I feel like I am on a boat being tossed about while Jesus just stands back and watches. Of course I know that isn't true. Jesus has been with me the whole time. He patiently waits for me to acknowledge His presence so He can part the flood of confusion inside my mind.

I had moments this week when I was completely leaning on Him, and then I had moments when I just sat in my bed saying to myself, "Lord, I don't know if You've noticed or not, but everything is crashing down around me and I'm drowning here. I'm tired; I can't do this anymore. I don't know what You want from me, but whatever it is, I don't have it!" God has always replied, though, with, "Amber, do you trust Me? Do you love Me more than anything? I'm in control of everything that is happening around you, and you do not need people, you need Me." "'For My thoughts are not your thoughts, neither are your ways My ways,' declares the LORD. 'For as the heavens are higher than the earth, so are My ways higher than your ways, and My thoughts than your thoughts. For as the rain and the snow come down from heaven, and do not return there without watering the earth and making it bear and sprout, and furnishing seed to the sower and bread to the eater; So shall My word be which goes forth from My mouth; It shall not return to Me empty, without accomplishing what I desire'" (Isaiah 55:8-11).

It's not about us at all. It's about the LORD and what He wants to accomplish in our lives! He cannot lie! Whatever He says, goes! If He were a liar, that'd go completely against His character. If He says He will accomplish what He so desires, He will. The question is will we allow Him to use us to further His Kingdom? God's ways are always higher than ours. I am convinced that God is moving in everyone's life; we choose whether or not to acknowledge His presence. He's in the trees, in the wind, in that close call with that semi, and in the smile from a stranger that made our day. We are His creation, and He loves us! He longs for us to love Him, for us to see the big picture.

Only the Holy Spirit can convict and bring about change. One day all will see that the only way to heaven is through Jesus Christ. To those who have chosen to truly trust Him and walk in His Truth, the reality of that statement is as clear as day. Jesus' precious blood bought us our freedom, and if we are disciples of Christ, it is our responsibility to share that freedom with others, even if we walk in the valley for years. He's still right there with us every step of the way, commanding us to spread the Good News.

"But even if you should suffer for the sake of righteousness, you are blessed; and do not fear their intimidation, and do not be troubled, but sanctify Christ as Lord in your hearts, always being ready to make a defense to everyone who asks you to give an account for the hope that is in you, yet with gentleness and reverence; and keep a good conscience so that in the thing in which you are slandered, those who revile your good behavior in Christ may be put to shame. For it is better, if God should will it so, that you suffer for doing what is right rather than for doing what is wrong. For Christ also died for sins once for all, the just for the unjust, so that He might bring us to God, having been put to death in the flesh, but made alive in the spirit" (I Peter 3:14-15).

There are millions who have no hope. They have their religion, but they don't feel truly free! They wonder why going to church every Sunday or going to confess their sins doesn't take away this gaping hole inside. It has been said that God created a hole inside of us all that was to be filled by Him and Him alone. If that's true, we're losing the battle if we try to look elsewhere, even to our churches. We aren't going to find any more of God inside a church building than we will in a bar. We put too much emphasis on the building and not enough on what God wants to do inside of us. He doesn't need a multimillion-dollar facility to draw people to Himself. He met a man named Saul, a man who absolutely despised Christians, on the dusty road to Damascus, and He turned him into one of the most influential people of all time. God made Paul's (formerly Saul) number one passion to spread the name of Christ instead of wiping it off the face of the earth.

God works in our hearts, and if we are half-heartedly serving Him it won't matter if we sit through a two-hour church service once a week or if we're a deacon. He'd rather we stay home and sleep in. God doesn't want our service because we feel obligated; He wants our hearts so He can teach us His ways, love us the way only He can, and give us a hope that no trial can take away. The only way He can do that, though, is if He has every facet of our lives. I don't claim to know everything about the Bible, but I do know that the overall theme of the Bible is those four words that I say all the time: **It's not about us.**

At the same time, though, it is about us. It's about giving Him everything we have and then experiencing the freedom that was purchased for us more than 2,000 years ago. We can do nothing to deserve it, but it's there, waiting for us to grab a hold of it. What are we afraid of? That we won't know what we're doing? I am sitting here only by the grace of God, and God alone. I am not perfect or even halfway close to it, but I do know that He is so holy, so worthy, and He wants each one of us. He wants us but we have to let go.

I've let go of a lot of things the past year, and every day I have to do it all over again. True surrender is not a one-time thing. It requires that we daily get on our knees and admit that God is indeed God and we're mere humans. We don't know His plan; we often don't see the big picture. Sometimes God just doesn't make sense to us. That's the way it's supposed to be. God wants us on our knees so He can strengthen us. His strength is perfected through our weakness. He's not looking for a résumé filled with years and years of Christian service. He's looking for Christ seekers, people who are willing to lay everything aside and follow after Him.

The price of freedom is much too high to ever pay, but that's why we have a Father filled with grace and forgiveness. We can't cheapen His grace and make it into a license to sin! God is far too holy just to allow that to occur. One day we will all fall flat on our faces and worship at Jesus' feet. But for now, we still have a choice. Will it be our way and temporal happiness or God's way and the freedom to soar in His arms?

FALSE ALARM 2:

June 19, 2006–Father's Day

- Called by Columbus Children's at 9:15 am, told to stay at home and wait for word if everything was "A Go."
- Although I was extremely tired, friends came over later that night to fellowship in my backyard.

June 19, 2005–This is it (Lord willing), Part 2

"In Christ alone will I glory"

—the apostle Paul

9:35 A.M.

Could day #53 be *the* day? Only God knows, but I was called this morning around 9:00 A.M., telling me they may have a possible donor. I'm just sitting here waiting for Dr. Astor to call me back to give me the go-ahead to come to Columbus. I won't know for sure whether or not I'm having my surgery until probably later on this afternoon.

I'm extremely excited but trying to remain a bit low-key about it, knowing it could very well be a false alarm again. I'm sure once things start rolling, my adrenaline will kick in. Right now, though, I'm fighting a migraine and not feeling well, so please pray for me. The car ride to Columbus may be a bit rough, considering how I'm feeling.

I may have new lungs by the end of the day, Father's Day, and there are no words to express what's going on in my mind and heart right now. I just want to encourage everyone to run the race with perseverance, setting aside everything that hinders. Even if we lose all our earthly possessions, He is far greater than anything this world could ever offer. We are to proclaim His mercy and His goodness wherever we go, never being ashamed of who He is and who we are in Christ. In life or death, we are His, and He guides our steps from here to eternity. We don't make excuses and say we'll live for Him tomorrow or next year. He doesn't need or want us only when it's convenient to us. We are to love Him, have hearts of servants, and enjoy the journey.

11:25 A.M.

It's been almost two-and-a-half hours since they called…still no word. My head's feeling a bit better, though. It's amazing how God provides exactly what we need and sometimes nothing more. My daddy would love for me to have my surgery today; he said it'd be the best Father's Day gift he's ever received.

12:23 P.M.

Well, it's a NO...sorry, guys. I'm not having my transplant today, but at least I get to spend the day with my dad and see my friends tonight. Dr. Astor said the donor was older and that they worked all night trying to make things work, but again, he feels that we can do better. I'm #1 in the state of Ohio for my blood type, so things shouldn't take too much longer.

That's all the news I have for now! Have faith, my friends. My day is coming!

JUNE 21, 2005–THE BODY OF CHRIST
DAY #55 ON THE LIST IS OVER!

Even though we didn't go to Columbus this time, it was still emotionally draining. The Lord is in complete control, though, and I know that just around the corner He has something bigger and better than any of us could ever dream. I don't know exactly what it is, but I have a feeling it's going to sweep all of us off our feet and make us fall facedown, praising our heavenly Father.

If we as the body of Christ are looking to Christ and Him alone, instead of striving solely for closer fellowship and keeping everyone happy, our praises will sound much sweeter to our Savior. We cannot be afraid to speak the truth to our fellow brothers and sisters in Christ, yet as I have learned, we must also remember that in the end we are responsible only for ourselves. It's a fine balance that I oftentimes have trouble defining, especially when it comes to the ones I love deeply. We must realize, though, that we can only do so much for someone who has fallen off track;

we can admonish them, but we cannot walk the path for them. The choices they make are exactly that, their choices.

I saw the Body in action Sunday night. I was sitting in my backyard on the grass with six other believers. We all told what the Lord had been teaching us over the past week or so. Five of them traveled to Canada last week to be leaders in a spiritual "boot camp," and it was amazing to see how God used the same experience to speak to each of them differently.

Our God is so personal. God doesn't speak to me the same way as He speaks to others, and that's OK. He doesn't want us to compare our Christian lives with each other's, wondering why we weren't called here like her or blessed like him.

I absolutely love I Corinthians 13:12, "For now we see in a mirror dimly, but then face to face; now I know in part then I will know fully just as I also have been fully known." The passage speaks about love in its fullest meaning, true love between God and man. I cannot wait until my faith will be made sight, and I will see Jesus just as He is. While on this earth, though, I walk by faith and not by sight (2 Corinthians 5:7) and daily surrender to the Spirit. He wants all of us, down to the inner core of who we are, the dark and the light; the good and the bad; the mundane and the crazy. He loves us, and He sent His Son to set us free from now to eternity. Why must so many live as if they're in chains when He has set us free (John 8:36)?

We are the Church. A multimillion-dollar building is a monetary investment. If Christians do not fill the place, it's nothing different than the warehouse down the street. The purpose of a body of believers coming together is to glorify the Father and exhort the Body. Christ isn't looking for perfect people to fill the seats. He built His church upon Peter, the same man who denied He ever knew Jesus. He only needs us to allow Him to perfect His strength through our weaknesses (2 Corinthians 12:9). When we, as a body, are engaged and focused solely on the kingdom and the task at hand, using the spiritual gifts He's given us, there's no telling what God can do with His church. How humble our Father in Heaven is. He could do everything by His own power, but He chooses to use *us* as His catalyst for change. It truly is an awesome responsibility and privilege to be a disciple of Jesus Christ.

Sacrifice & Freedom

I'm a firm believer that there truly is freedom in sacrificing all to the One who gave all. As my journey continues, these are more entries of wrestling with life and death and gaining truths from His Word.

"When Christ calls a man, he bids him come and die."
—Dietrich Bonehoffer[11]

JULY 4, 2005–JUST ASK
DAY #68 ON THE LIST IS OVER!

This weekend has definitely been emotionally trying. The fact is this, I *need* my surgery, I know it and so does God.

He knows that it's the 4th of July weekend, the number one time of year for traffic accidents; meaning donors are usually plentiful. He knows. He doesn't need me to remind Him. Yet my humanity cannot help but want to scream sometimes.

I just wish I could say that one-hundred percent of the time I'm completely at peace with my circumstances, that nothing is bothering me. I don't have to be able to say that, though, for God to work through me. In fact, in His Word He says that His strength is perfected through our weaknesses. Admitting to the Lord that there are moments when I feel completely overwhelmed, moments I feel like I not only can't breathe physically but spiritually/emotionally as well, are the most freeing. Jesus willingly offers to carry our burdens or even carry us, if necessary. He already knows when we're over our heads, and He's just waiting for me to ask for His help. If we can't come up with the words to say, the Spirit promises to intercede for us.

So tonight, as I get ready to go to bed, I will remember that my God is sovereign, holy, and loving. He will provide in His perfect timing. It's so hard to find the balance between making jokes about "the top five pick-up lines to say to eligible lung donors" and realizing that someone will indeed lose his or her life in this process. I am praying for my donor and their family, as the last thing I want to do is dishonor that person and their life. That would never be my intention. Whoever they are, they are already very special to all of us. God be with them wherever they are tonight.

Father, may you convict me when I fail to realize just how much You've given me. I'm sorry for all the times I haven't gone to You first with my fears and aspirations. Without You, I am nothing. But because of Jesus and His sacrifice, I can live in true *freedom. The freedom we have even here in the United States pales in comparison to the freedom I find in Jesus, Father. You are my song, my joy, and the love of my life. You are my God, and I am Yours. So hold me now; I need You more than words can say. Have*

Your way with me and make me a pure reflection of Your glory. None of me and all of You, my King.

JULY 6, 2005–COMFORT
DAY #70 ON THE LIST IS OVER!

Today, the first thought I had was something to the effect of, "I can't do this anymore. I'm sick and tired of being sick and tired. Thanks, God. This has been fun and all, but I'm tired of the Ferris wheel and monotony. Get me off this stupid ride." That was a wonderful greeting I gave my heavenly Father. Part of me wants to say I'm not even sorry I said it, but yet I am. I absolutely loathe myself when I get like that.

We have been given so much, and we don't even realize it. I'm not talking about us as Americans, but us as the Body of Christ. "Who shall separate us from the love of Christ? Shall tribulation, or distress, or persecution, or famine, or nakedness, or peril, or sword? But in all these things we overwhelmingly conquer through Him who loved us. For I am convinced that neither death, nor life, nor angels, nor principalities, nor things present, nor things to come, nor powers, nor height, nor depth, nor any other created thing, shall be able to separate us from the love of God, which is in Christ Jesus our Lord" (Romans 8:35, 37-39).

Christ's love cannot be overpowered by anything on this earth. I'm constantly reminded of this verse as well. "For now we see in a mirror dimly, but then face to face; now I know in part, but then I shall know fully just as I also have been fully known. But now abide faith, hope, love, these three; but the greatest of these is love" (1 Corinthians 13:12-13).

I cannot wait until my Faith is made sight, and I see Jesus face-to-face. The partial will be done away with (1 Corinthians 13:10) and He will stand in all His glory.

The Word says it best:

"Grace to you and peace from God our Father and the Lord Jesus Christ. Blessed *be* the God and Father of our Lord Jesus Christ, the Father of mercies and God of all comfort, who comforts us in all our affliction so that we will be able to comfort those who are in any affliction with the comfort with which we ourselves are comforted by God. For just as the sufferings of Christ are ours in abundance, so also our comfort is abundant through Christ. But if we are afflicted, it is for your comfort and salvation; or if we are comforted, it is for your comfort, which is effective in the patient enduring of the same sufferings which we also suffer; and our hope for you is firmly grounded, knowing that as you are sharers of our sufferings, so also you are *sharers* of our comfort."

—2 Corinthians 1:2-7

My God is the same today, tomorrow, and forever. The same God who comforted Paul and Timothy comforts me. I don't need scientific proof that God exists. The liquid peace that comes over me so quickly is enough proof for me. Thank God, I am free!

JULY 11, 2005
Author's Note:

Although it appeared I would be, I was not the first person transplanted at Columbus Children's Hospital. In fact, Emily DeArdo was the first person to receive a double lung transplant at the facility. At the age of twenty-three, Emily received her miracle and continues to do well.

Reflections

Melissa:

I have known Amber Metz all my life. Back when we were younger, my mother would babysit her and her younger sister on a regular basis, so of course I saw her all the time. Through those years, if I can be honest, I couldn't really stand her. I saw her as this little girl who was invading my turf. Years went by and our relationship began to change. I no longer saw her as an enemy, but as a friend. Around my junior year of high school, Amber and I became extremely close through our leadership in our chapter of *Teens for Christ*, and also through our experiences with our boyfriends at the time.

Through these past few years I have seen an enormous change in Amber, first through her health and second through her spiritual growth. I think for years I had been pretty numb to Amber's physical condition. Ever since she was a little girl I have seen her popping pills and producing the scariest cough, and yet thought nothing of it. Watching her as her cystic fibrosis grew to the point of possible death, I was faced with the reality of her sickness and the possibility of losing one of my best friends.

The day I received the call from Amber that she was on her way to the hospital, I was at my boyfriend's house. As I sat there hearing her calm yet excited voice telling me that she was on her way for her lungs, I could not keep back the tears. I told her that I loved her and would be praying and that everything would be okay. I got off the phone only to start crying to my boyfriend, because deep down it was a harsh reality that I could be saying good-bye to my friend. We proceeded to get together with his family and pray for her. It was a long night for me, because it is in my nature to worry, and worry I did. I trusted God that He was in control and no matter what happened, it was in His will. When the news came that she had made it through, I was so happy, because like others I was extremely happy for her that she would no longer have trouble taking a breath, but that she could be normal, at least as normal as Amber can be.

Seeing Amber first hand, I understand the struggle she had the year before she received her lungs. She was tired. When I would take her to the doctor, it felt like I was taking an elderly woman because of the oxygen tanks and her inability to open doors and climb stairs. As a friend, it is an extremely painful experience to watch someone go through that and also a humbling experience to care for her. Through all of these trials, I saw the birth of an Amber I had never known. She was always so positive; she trusted God and she never gave up. She saw the possibility of death looking her in the face and she was ready to go.

Being only twenty at the time myself, it was amazing to me to see my nineteen-year-old best friend in her weak state, encouraging me in my walk with Christ, always pushing me forward. When I think of Amber and her new ministry in life, I think of Esther and how God carries out His will through His people. I know He has chosen to carry out His will through Amber for such a time as this. Amber may not have the prospect of being on earth for many years, none of us does, but she is determined to do what her Father has called her to do, in the time He has given her.

I am so proud of Amber and I look up to her strength and her bravery. I'm thankful for our friendship and love during the hard days when she encouraged me to forge ahead. I thank her for the honesty to push me to be the spiritual leader that I can be. I love her, my friend and "my twin".

JULY 16, 2005–SALVATION
DAY #80 ON THE LIST IS OVER!

I want to be like Paul (the disciple in the Bible). I want to be able to say that I am content in everything and that God's agenda is always at the forefront of my mind. At the same time, I am reminded that Paul's DNA was made out of the same material as mine, and I'm sure he had his moments too. But that's no excuse! I can still be thankful, and I am, for everything the Lord has so graciously bestowed upon my family and me.

I may want to be *like* Paul, but I don't want to be Paul. I want to be Amber Nicole Metz, because that's who God has called me to be. He has called others to be themselves. He's not asking us to be someone else. God is calling us out of our sin to live a life praising Him through our relationship with Jesus Christ. We bring Him glory in our own special way using the talents and passions God gave us when He knit each of us in our mother's womb.

Think of an Uncle Sam poster minus Uncle Sam. Instead, Jesus Christ, God made flesh, is saying "I want you for the kingdom of God." His eyes are piercing yet loving at the same time, and we cannot help but feel drawn into His presence and His passion. We will have to sacrifice, but giving Jesus everything we have will be our greatest honor, and our fellow countrymen will thank us when they see what He's done for us when they too decide to join the ranks and fight in the Lord's Army. After all, there is a battle going on between the forces of good and evil every single day, whether we realize it or not.

To rise in rank in this army, we must remain humble and teachable. No smart aleck, pompous private is going to impress anybody. One who helps his brother and remains steadfast, though, will catch the eye of his commanding officer quickly, allowing trust to be formed and more responsibility to be granted. Such is the way when it comes to our walk with Christ. He will not trust us with the bigger issues if He cannot trust us with the smaller ones. He will not put up with pride.

When it comes to humility, God trumps us all. No matter how humble we may be, even after accepting Christ and learning to walk in His truth, God's display of the purest form of humility should astound us. The Father could have displayed His glory any way He chose. But He chose to use us, humans with raw emotions and more mistakes than we'd like to admit. God didn't have to send His Son, Jesus, to die for our sins and buy back our freedom for now and eternity, but He did. He could have sentenced us all to death under the Old Law and watched us burn in Hell, but He didn't. He is Love, after all.

Any thirty-second commercial or 270-page self-help book that claims to have the answers to all of our problems is nothing short of just another one of Satan's scheming lies. Satan and his angels will do anything in their power to defeat us, to kick us while we're down. Satan has no power over the Trinity, and Christ holds the keys to death and hell. But Satan is roaming the earth and seeking to devour whomever he can destroy.

He is just and worthy of all our praise. He doesn't need our permission to fulfill His will, to turn our lives upside down for the good of His Kingdom. He's God! He doesn't need us telling Him what we want or even what we need. He already knows! On the other hand, isn't it wonderful to know that God wants to hear from His children about their wants and desires, about what makes them tick, and what fills their hearts with joy? He wants to align our wills to His, to show us His freedom is better than anything money can buy.

God is not a liar, and His Word will not return void. God is by definition "Love." At the same time, He is just and holy, so holy, in fact, that He cannot allow sin to enter His presence. That's why He sent Jesus to die on a cross. God even turned His back on Him in the process because God could not bear to see the sin on His own Son's back. Jesus didn't stay in the grave, though! On the third day He rose again and stood in the presence of humans once more. The prophecies of old were proven true, and the world had a Savior in Jesus Christ, the hope of glory. In God's Word it clearly says that eternal separation from God is the punishment for not accepting His Son, Jesus Christ. We will all stand before the Lord one day, and for the ones who have not accepted, they will hear "Depart from me. I never knew you." That's why it is so very important that the ones of us who have been *blessed* to know the Truth share the Truth with others who are in desperate need, putting them before ourselves and being concerned for their welfare.

Father,

Help me to continue to be moldable as clay, allowing You to make me into whomever You would have me to be. Use me, teach me, show me, and guide me, Lord. I want so desperately to be where You want me to be. Break my pride, and empty me of all the useless things I hold onto. Help me to continue to have laser-light focus, staying on track with what You need me to do, always being ready to have an answer for the hope that is within me and never asking for anything out of conceit or for my own self-worth. All for You, my precious King. You are my Adonai.

JULY 25, 2005–LIVING STONES
DAY #88 ON THE LIST IS OVER!

I've been constantly thinking about how I am *not* God, nor am I expected to understand everything He's done, is doing, or will do in the future. God has *so* much for us, if we'll just shut up (for lack of better words) and allow Him to speak to us (Galatians 4:4-7).

God has made me more than a conqueror through Jesus Christ, my Lord (Romans 8:37). Because of His precious blood, nothing (even my ignorance) will be able to separate me from His love (Romans 8:38-39). Those of us who profess Jesus Christ as our Lord and Savior become living temples of the Holy Spirit;

we've been bought with a price, and we're called to glorify God in our bodies (1 Corinthians 6:19-20).

"And coming to Him, as to a living stone, rejected by men, but choice and precious in the sight of God, you also, as living stones, are being built up as a spiritual house for a holy priesthood, to offer up spiritual sacrifices acceptable to God through Jesus Christ" (I Peter 2:4-5). Jesus Christ is the Lamb who died for you and for me. "For we also once were foolish ourselves, disobedient, deceived, enslaved to various lusts and pleasures, spending our life in malice and envy, hateful, hating one another. But when the kindness of God our Savior and *His* love for mankind appeared, He saved us, not on the basis of deeds that we have done in righteousness, but according to His mercy, by the washing of regeneration and renewing by the Holy Spirit, whom He poured out upon us richly through Jesus Christ our Savior, that being justified by His grace we would be made heirs according to the hope of eternal life" (Titus 3:3-7).

We don't need the High Priest anymore to enter the Holy of Holies for us on the Day of Atonement to offer the peoples' sacrifice for their sins. Jesus has become our high priest (Hebrews 4:14-16) and *we*, ourselves, have become the Holy of Holies, if indeed we know Jesus as our Savior. What an amazing, mind-boggling thought!

As I press on in my journey, I'm realizing that I'm never going to have all the answers or anywhere near one-tenth of one-percent of them. All I have to do is just be me, being in love with God and bringing Him glory through my relationship with Jesus Christ, my Healer, Redeemer, Messiah, First Love, and Coming King. With God's help, I think I'm truly becoming myself, fulfilling the divine calling only He could have placed on my life, learning to travel the high road in everything, holding on to His hand and walking into the unknown, fearless of what may befall me.

We don't have to have it all together before we can fall at the feet of grace. He's waiting for us to realize that we are nothing without Him but *so* much more than we could ever imagine with Him.

AUGUST 2005

- Had been in bed for over eight months
- Been listed since April 27, 2005, and had already experienced two false alarms
- Fev1 dipped yet again
- Oxygen concentrator turned up to 3.0-3.5 L
- Strength was waning and was hardly able to leave my room
- Friends were preparing to leave to go back to college.
- I wondered if it would be the last time I saw them this side of heaven.

CHAPTER SIX

Desperation: Part One

"I am convinced that God is not found in the ease of our accommodation but in the level of our desperation for Him."

—Anonymous

AUGUST 5, 2005–DAY #100: NEW AGAIN
DAY #100 ON THE LIST IS OVER...

I have to remind myself that no matter how high our little countdown (count up) goes, it doesn't change the fact that God's has always been watching over me. I'm not waiting for God to show up, He never went anywhere to begin with! God has been there from the beginning of time (Genesis 1:1). In fact, our human concept of time doesn't even apply to our heavenly Father. He's not contained by space, time, or any other method we try to wrap our minds around to explain Him.

One day, the Lord Jesus Christ will return in all His glory (Mark 13:26), and the dead in Christ will rise first, followed by the ones who remain, being caught up in the clouds and living forever with the Lord (1 Thessalonians 4:17). I don't pretend to understand everything (or much of anything) to do with the book of Revelation, but I do know that all of us were created for so much more than what this fallen earth has to offer. There is so much going on around us that we will undoubtedly never be aware, no matter how close we draw to the Savior's side.

The whole creation has been groaning (Romans 8:22) since the fall. Something's off, and not only do our souls know it, so do the trees, the birds, the mountains, the oceans. In Jesus, though, God is putting it all back together.

Jesus promises to make all things new! (Revelation 21:5). His birth, death, and resurrection were about much more than just human salvation. I'm just beginning to see that for myself. I was reading a book last night that pointed out this fact. I put the book down and just sat there for a long while. All of a sudden, it began to make sense. It doesn't make perfect sense to me yet, because when I think about freedom in Christ and the reason the Son of God came to this earth, I hadn't really thought about how He did it not only for humans. Jesus is coming back for His bride (the Church). I don't know when, or if it'll be before or after the tribulation, but I do know that He's coming for His children, to set up the new heaven and new earth. The old will be done away with, and the brokenness the world has felt for so very long will finally be mended by the One who has set us free. We will live forever in His glorious light, worshipping our Savior, Jesus Christ. Our bodies will be glorified, and He will wipe away every tear, defeating death. I can't wait. I want to see Jesus for who He really is. I long for the ability to worship Him the way I should, to love Him with the parts of my soul that I still guard without even consciously knowing it.

At the same time, I *can* wait, because I've already bought into my freedom here on earth. I'm not afraid of death. I say along with Paul that, "to be absent with the body is to be present with the Lord" (2 Corinthians 5:8). I'm a child of the living God, and no matter what happens to me, nothing can separate me from the love of God (Romans 8:39).

I have so very much to learn, and I want so very badly to be used. I've learned that sacrifice is crucial to the journey, to finding the joy that is in Christ alone. I know that it is only when I lose everything that I will truly see the beauty of giving all to the One who gave all.

Redemption hasn't been completed in its entirety. Creation itself was subjected to futility in hope that the creation will be set free from its slavery to corruption into the freedom of the glory of the children of God (Romans 8:21). Rocks were created to glorify the Father, and so were we. My body is only an outer shell for an eternal being, a soul that will live forever. Once we are dead and gone, there are no re-dos, no "get-out-of-jail-free cards". We all go around once, and it's during the time we spend on earth that we make decisions that will determine where we go for every second of eternity.

The Holy Spirit is the only one who can move in someone's life. As it says in 1 Thessalonians 5:19, do *not* quench the Holy Spirit. We allow God to move among us, through us. For some reason God chose humans to fulfill His purposes, to spread His truth. He sent His Son to pay for our sins, making us the righteousness of God in the process. He gave us the Holy Spirit as a guide, and now He's sending us out to make disciples in his name. I hear all the time about how I should believe in God, but I have also thought about how God believes in me. He loves me and He's called me to something far more spectacular than the boring, mundane life that used to satisfy me before I knew Christ.

When I first came to know the Lord I was so excited. It's funny how that feeling fades. I thought the more I read my Bible or the more I prayed, the closer I was going to get to God. That was my problem. During that time I was frustrated and even angry at times with the lack of progress I seemed to be making. Now I've learned that when God said delight in His law and in Him (Proverbs 23:26), He meant what He said. I can't really delight in something if I'm coming at it with an agenda. If I'm reading my Bible for the sole purpose of fulfilling my Christian duty, well then I'm no better than the Pharisees. God isn't looking for Bible scholars. He's looking for willing hearts that are desperately seeking Him with everything that they have.

I love myself so much more, though, and because of that, I am able to see the power of Christ working in me in a clearer, more concise way. I don't focus so much on what I don't know or what I can't do, but more on who I am in Christ and the power of His Spirit working within me. Jesus is my sole reason for living. My ego should be beaten to the ground so that I can glorify Christ in all things. At the *same* time, though, Christians should not deny who they are in Christ! Doing so just brings the attention back to us and away from Christ's work in our lives.

> "… *Very* few people in our world are offering anything worth dying for. Most of the messages we receive are about how to make life easier. The call of Jesus goes the other direction. It's about making our lives more difficult. It is going out of our way to be more generous and disciplined and loving and free. It is refusing to escape and become numb to and check out of this broken, fractured world. And so we are embracing the high demands of Jesus' call to be one of his disciples. We are honest about it. We want our friends to know up front that the costs are high, which is what is so appealing about Jesus-his vision for life takes everything we have."
>
> —Rob Bell in *Velvet Elvis: Repainting the Christian Faith*[12]

Author's Note:

While I use this quote from *Velvet Elvis: Repainting the Christian Faith* by Rob Bell, I do not agree with all of the theological conclusions he has come to and subsequently alluded to in his book. I think as the Church, it is crucial that we embrace the incarnation of Jesus but, at the same time, we cannot lose the doctrines that exalt our Lord and display who He is, the King of Kings and the Lord of Lords, One who satisfied the *wrath* of God and bore the shame of the cross for you and for me. Amen.[13]

AUGUST 9, 2005–DAYS #101-105: ONWARD DAYS #101, 102, 103, 104 & 105 ARE OVER!

I never thought I would make it to day #100, and now that I've passed it, I find myself somewhat at a loss for words. I used to get all excited when the phone rang, thinking that maybe this was *the* call, but after a while the excitement subsided and I was no longer jumpy every time someone called.

At times, I feel like I'm being torn apart. The fully conscious part of me knows that God is in complete control, that He is being glorified through every second of my waiting, and that I'll be thankful for these lessons in patience later in life. The other part of me, the extremely tired/somewhat foggy in my thinking part, keeps trying to convince me that I have full right to feel sorry for myself. How many nineteen-year-olds are saying goodbye to their friends, fully knowing there is a very real possibility that this could be the last time they see them before God calls them Home? How many have planned their funerals, watched the world pass them by from their bedroom window for months, and felt this internal clock that keeps telling them that time is of the essence?

I know that it's wrong to think this way, and honestly I don't think about many of those points very often. If I did so, I would have far less emotional and spiritual energy than I do now. I have to be honest and open about how I'm feeling, though, or I would not be true to myself or to my Father in Heaven. I'm not perfect, and I am constantly relying on Him to give me the strength, courage, and determination to keep going, to keep moving into the unknown. I honestly don't know how people who don't know my Lord and Savior go through life, especially if they're faced with a crisis.

I've had the mindset before that *I* didn't need anything, that I had everything under control. Even though I knew Christ, I still thought I could get by pretty much on my own—that He was available if I got in a really tough spot that I couldn't handle. I thought if I could manage, what was the use in bothering Him? How foolish of me!

Jesus Christ *is* the sole reason we have the ability to face tomorrow. Even if we don't acknowledge that truth on this side of heaven, the fact still remains the same. Just because we don't admit that something's true doesn't change the fact of whether or not it is. I think it takes more energy to not believe in the Redemption and the world being God-centered than it does to be a believer. Even if someone says it's impossible to know if there is a God, that still takes some capacity of belief.

In any case, I realized a long time ago that there is such a joy in the journey, of knowing that I, Amber Metz, can't do this. I was never created to do this on my own. The moment I figured that out was the day I got my freedom back. Jesus paid my debt, tore the veil, and now He leads me down a narrow path filled with adventure, danger, and mystery. This was what I was created to do.

I'm doing all I can to stay positive, but sometimes I fall and I find myself swimming in an ocean of emotion, begging for a life raft. The only flotation device that is going to be able to hold me is my personal relationship with Jesus Christ. No human being will ever be able to satisfy the deepest longings of my soul, nor was any person ever intended to do so. Jesus Christ is still the same—yesterday, today and forever (Hebrews 13:8).

With Jesus, we don't have to make decisions on our own. The answers don't show up on the walls of our houses, and He doesn't speak to us in burning bushes (not that He couldn't), but He's speaking nonetheless. God is not in the hustle and bustle of society. To find God, one must look in the solitude. "The LORD your God is in your midst, a victorious warrior. He will exult over you with joy, He will be quiet in His love, He will rejoice over you with shouts of joy" (Zephaniah 3:17).

God is looking for people who will shut their mouths, get away, and just listen to what He has to say. Prayer is not just a one-way conversation, no matter how much it appears to be at times. God is speaking to His people. I've never heard an audible voice, but when the Holy Spirit moves, in the way only the Spirit can, you know. There are no words that can really describe it. "Behold, how happy is the man whom God reproves, so do not despise the discipline of the Almighty. For He inflicts pain, and gives relief; He wounds, and His hands *also* heal" (Job 5:17-19).

God will discipline us, because if He didn't He wouldn't be true to His nature. At the same time, God is a God of mercy, grace, and love. He may seem like a paradox to some, but I have found that there is beauty beyond compare in His infinite characteristics.

The wave of my friends leaving for college has already begun, and I'm trying real hard to put on my brave face and just take it in stride. But I'm human, and it has not been so easy. I know that God is going with them to Minnesota, Georgia, and everywhere else they'll end up by the end of August when the last ones pack up and head out.

Sometimes, I just need to step back and get out of the moment. I get lost in the emotion, in the here and now. Being focused on the here and now is usually a good thing, but when it causes me to lose sight of all that God has in store, it's best to keep my eyes forward. I may not know what's ahead, but I do know that He does, and that's all that matters. He has brought me this far, proving Himself to be so faithful, time and time again. I have no doubt that He will lead me safely to the other side of this trial. I sure don't want to miss my chance to change the world for His glory.

I get so very lost sometimes and far from where I should be, but I'm so thankful that He's always there to bring me back to reality, even if it appears so harsh to me at times. My rose-colored glasses have begun to come off, and I'm beginning to realize that I'm far from the end of all this, that surgery is only the beginning of a long recovery. I'm ready, though, to get out of this valley and start climbing a mountain. The sooner I get to the top, the sooner I will be able to see just how much He has had in store for me all along. I cannot lose sight of the journey or all the ground I've already covered will have been worthless. I can't move forward without a clear understanding of where I'm at now and where I've been. Come quickly, Lord Jesus. Show me what You want me to do in all situations, big and small. I'm oh so tired, but oh so willing to keep going, as long as You continue to carry me. If it would be Your will, though, I'd love to come down and run on my own two feet.

AUGUST 16, 2005–DAYS #110-112: PENGUINS DAYS #110, 111 & 112 ON THE LIST ARE OVER!

The Lord has laid *so* much on my heart the past couple days, and I'm excited to share. He's also been giving me an odd amount of strength the past few days, allowing me to get out of my room a few times and spend quality time out and about with friends before they leave for college.

I have been blessed to realize the urgency of the gospel. God has given me a heart for discipleship of believers and, at times it's hard to not come across forcefully. I love the Father with all that I have and ever will be, and I long for others to feel the freedom I've found in His Son, Jesus Christ. I can't help but tell of His excellent greatness (Ephesians 1:18-23). I've been down the other road, the road that leads to mediocrity and a feeling of emptiness, and I never want to go back.

The Father took away everything I had to show me that He is all I will ever need and more. God blew apart the box I had Him in, and I know now that my hope and stay is Christ and Christ alone. No degree of health, no amount of love from others, no profession – nothing – will satisfy the thirst within me. I want to drink from only the Life Giver's well, forsaking everything else that promises to fulfill me. So I'm passionate about where I've been, where I am now, and the plans God has for me in my future. May my life be a reflection of His glory, a constant reminder to a lost, dying world of the hope they too can find in Christ. Jesus Christ's freedom is filled with grace.

In Titus 2, verses 11-15, Paul says, "For the grace of God has appeared, bringing salvation to all men, instructing us to deny ungodliness and worldly desires and to live sensibly, righteously and godly in the present age, looking for the blessed hope and the appearing of the glory of our great God and Savior, Christ Jesus; who gave Himself for us to redeem us from every lawless deed and purify for Himself a people for His own possession, zealous for good deeds. These things speak and exhort and reprove with all authority. Let no one disregard you."

It is only by God's grace that we have sweet communion with Him here on earth and for eternity in heaven. Jesus is the way, the truth, and the life (John 14:6). Without God's grace, we're doomed to a life apart from our Creator. We're "East of Eden," and the effects of the fall still stand. We need a Savior, and we were given one in Jesus Christ, God personified in the flesh. "For if by the transgression of the one [Adam], death reigned through the one, much more those who receive the abundance of grace and of the gift of righteousness will reign in life through the One, Jesus Christ. So then as through one transgression there resulted condemnation to all men, even so through one act of righteousness there resulted justification of life to all men. For as through the one man's disobedience the many were made sinners, even so through the obedience of the One the many will be made righteous. And the Law came in so that the transgression might increase; but where sin increased, grace abounded all the more, so that, as sin reigned in death, even so grace might reign through righteousness to eternal life through Jesus Christ our Lord"(Romans 5:17-21).

Grace is something I don't understand. My mind tells me that there must be something I have to do for God to love me. The thought of God loving me just as much now as He did back when I hadn't even acknowledged Jesus' death and resurrection that bought me my freedom, or the power of the Holy Spirit working in my life, is beyond me. Even then God loved me much more so than I will ever be able to comprehend. That's the beauty of grace. "For you know the grace of our Lord Jesus Christ, that though He was rich, yet for your sake He became poor, so that you through His poverty might become rich" (2 Corinthians 8:9).

Jesus came and became nothing by earthly standards, taking the form of a bond-servant (Phil. 2:5-11), so that we could take part in the fullness of Christ (John 1:16). Jesus came to heal the brokenhearted and set the captives free (Isaiah 61:1). Nothing we will ever do will make us worthy of God's unmerited favor in our lives, yet there He is, calling out to us, wanting us to realize that there's so much more going on than we could ever imagine. It's not about doctrine, religion, or duty, it's about a relationship with Jesus Christ, one that requires sacrifice on both sides. He already proved Himself worthy more than 2,000 years ago when He died on Calvary for us. Redemption is already in progress. He's bidding us to come and die to ourselves, take up our cross, and follow after Him (Matthew 16:24).

Psalm 37:4 (kjv) says, "Delight thyself also in the Lord; and he shall give thee the desires of thine heart." I am praying that my desires are truly aligning with His. But at the same time, I get scared that I'm just a dreamer who dreams dreams that are too big, that maybe I haven't truly laid some things down. It has been hard because the Lord has been showing me so much grace, allowing me to just delight in Him. I have felt so loved by Him, and at the same time I've been afraid the whole time that I've not been anywhere near where I should be, spiritually speaking. It seems He just keeps bringing me back to the fact that I have learned to trust Him, and that I do want His will for my life. He is in control. I feel that the Lord can and does speak to us through our emotions. It's a long, hard road, but He's there to guide me every step of the way as long as I just keep moving toward Him. He's pursuing all of us, longing to dance with us if we'd just slow down and listen to the music.

One night I went to see *March of the Penguins* at the movies, and I had no idea the Lord would use that film to speak to me. The audience gets to watch a group of emperor penguins for a nine-month period. From the long seventy-mile journey from the ocean to the breeding ground, to the birth of the baby penguins, to the subsequent trips back to the ocean by mother and father penguin for food, it was absolutely amazing. God showed me through that movie that if He created these creatures and takes care of them, then how much more does He love and promise to take care of me (Matthew 6:26)? Even the penguins are longing for the redemption (Romans 8:8-25). They have to travel miles longer than they used to because the ice in Antarctica is constantly shifting, making their journey treacherous. With minus-eighty degree temperatures, these creatures roam around on the ice pack, following their God-given instincts that get them to safety every time, provided they can withstand the harsh conditions. So as the story goes on the penguins know something is up, something has gone haywire, and it is getting harder to fulfill their duties to make the breeding journey their meaning for existence. They, too, were created to bring God glory. That is their meaning for existence, and when they're doing what God's called them to do, they fulfill their calling.

Doesn't Christ promise to be our compass as long as we are in tune with His agenda? I don't want to trust my instincts, but I do want to trust Christ and keep believing in that perfect peace that truly does surpass all understanding (Phil. 4:7). Even when everything around us is crumbling, He still loves us and calls us out for something greater than ourselves, something magical, something intimately ours—a relationship with His Son, Jesus Christ. He's still teaching me, though, and I long to know more tomorrow than I do today.

AUGUST 21, 2005–DAYS #113-116: I CAN'T BUT I KNOW HE CAN DAYS #113-116 ON THE LIST ARE OVER!

1:30 A.M.

I had a bad day today! Can I just get that off my chest? Will you think less of me if I do? Should I even care? At the same time, I know God is in complete control of my situation, even though part of me feels as if everything around me is spinning. I'm not saying my God is not holy, righteous, loving, and all I will ever need; He is everything to me, so much more than I could ever deserve, ask, or be able to wrap my finite mind around. He is Creator (Genesis 1:1), Sustainer (Psalm 55:22), I AM (Ex. 3:14), the Word (John 1:1), Alpha & Omega (Rev. 1:8), and, most personal of all, mine. Yes, God is mine and I am *His;* no bad day could ever change that fact.

A lot of things just hit me today all at once, and I found my mind couldn't come up with answers fast enough for the countless questions my mind was coming up with, leaving me feeling lost at sea. All along, though, I knew there were no answers to most of my questions, other than one, trust Him. Those two words have hit me squarely in the eyes a thousand times over the course of the past year. I don't feel the Holy Spirit nudging me with the question, "Do you trust Me?" as much as I used to, but I honestly think it's because I have learned to trust Him. Every day is a journey, and I'm constantly learning new lessons. I've found that my Lord is faithful and good, and so worthy of our praise.

6:10 P.M.

I stopped writing last night in the middle of my train of thought because I was exhausted in so many ways. I was physically, emotionally, and spiritually spent. I couldn't for the life of me come up with words to convey any of the thoughts and emotions that were accompanied by tears that burned my face like hot embers.

Even though I wasn't questioning God's ever-present hand in my life, I was feeling so small, so defeated, and so unworthy of the ministry He's given me. On top of that, I didn't even want to be where I am. I wanted to be back in Cedarville, or in Georgia or Minnesota with close friends. Or, better yet, just anywhere but here.

Most of my friends are now off at their respective colleges, and if I had known three months ago that I would still be sitting here in my room at the end of summer without a new set of lungs, I probably would have honestly had an emotional breakdown. I'm so thankful the Lord is the only one who is omniscient, because I certainly wouldn't have wanted to know how the summer was going to transpire. I pretty much banked on my life being much different at this stage. But He really does know what He's doing with all of our lives, if we'd only learn to trust Him.

I've learned so much about what it means to truly trust Him. Over the past year I've seen my life turned upside down. I lost my health, my security, and everything that I ever held dear on this earth and found that there is nothing here on this earth that could ever make me want to stay. I, Lord willing, will be better sometime in the future. But even then, I know my allegiance will be to my heavenly Father, for it is only because of Him that I will even have the opportunity to breathe again. I would say embrace life again, but I think I've actually been able to embrace life so much more than I ever have before, laying aside everything that hinders me and keeping my eyes on Jesus, the author and finisher of my faith (Hebrews 12:2). May I never forget where I've been and what He's brought me through. I don't care about anything but His glory. Whatever I can do to bring people into the kingdom, I'm more than game.

That's how I feel today. Last night, though, I was tired of feeling like I'm 102, like the world is passing me by. I want to be able to breathe, to feel beautiful again, to express what's truly on my heart without feeling like I have to pass everything through this censor called "Would this be the most profitable for you and others?" Last night I felt like I was being buried alive. Satan had stolen all my joy, and I found myself wondering if I had the strength to go on.

I can't go on living feeling defeated, and I'm so thankful that I don't have to because of the blood of the Lamb. He has made me free (Galatians 5:1). He has rescued me out of my dark pit and given me back my joy. It is only because of Him that I have anything at all. If only we, as Christians, would believe that Christ is in us! (Col.1: 24-29). I don't have to do anything but ask for His guidance and lay down my will, and He will always do what is best for me and for the kingdom in the process.

May I give up everything, allowing Him to refine me and make me fully His. I boast not of my talents or my strength, but of the strength of my Lord Jesus Christ and the work of His Holy Spirit in my life. May I keep my gaze fixed upward (Colossians 3:2), remembering that "when Christ, who is our life, is revealed, then you also will be revealed with Him in glory" (Col. 3:4). Christ, who is our life. My life is not my own. Christ is my life, and I lay myself down as a bondservant to Him.

That does not mean I won't have days where I'm discouraged. We wrestle not, though, against people, money, or anything else we try to blame it on. Satan is the father of lies (John 8:44), and it's his goal to make us, as children of the Living God, to feel as if we're alone and trapped. If we give him an inch, he'll try to take a mile. So may we put on the whole armor of God, so that we may withstand the schemes of the devil (Eph.6:11). Jesus is the same yesterday, today, and forever (Hebrews 13:8), and the word of God is "living and active and sharper than any two-edged sword, and piercing as far as the division of soul and spirit, of both joints and marrow, and able to judge the thoughts and intentions of the heart" (Hebrews 4:12).

AUGUST 26, 2005–DAYS #117-121: WHAT'S SO AMAZING ABOUT GRACE? DAYS #117, 118, 119, 120 & 121 ARE OVER!

I'm not feeling well tonight. May He grant me grace as I, just a simple servant, try to pen the thoughts and emotions that have been tugging on my heartstrings. I have found myself so much more in love with my Savior the past few days, and I cannot help but be floored by the incredible beauty that comes from the pain. I'm learning that while traveling the journey one does die, but at the same time, one truly lives!

God is teaching me *so* much about grace. I absolutely love it! I was sitting here last night at 4:00 A.M. reading Philip Yancey's *What's So Amazing About Grace,* with hot tears streaming down my face.

God's Word says they will know us by the way we love each other (John 13:35). I cannot help but think we have lost the art of grace, that I have lost the art of grace. I think that right there is the lesson that God has been showing me over the past couple of weeks. I do put so much emphasis on truth and standing for it and not backing down, but at the same time, grace is so very crucial to our faith. Truth does set us free, but without grace there wouldn't even be any truth to begin with. Jesus is grace, He's truth, and most of all, He is love.

The Father didn't need me, yet He created me and then called me out of my sin and into His family so that I can spend the rest of my life delighting in my maker (Psalm 37:4) and making my lifesong all about Him. Grace is so full and free for us as Christians.

Jesus came so that we might have life and life to the full (John 10:10). May we hold fast to the Scripture, knowing that Jesus took on the sins of the world and offered up Himself as a servant for us. Through Jesus, God set in motion His plan of making all things new. It may just seem like lyrics from an old hymn, but amazing grace truly did save us! We are no longer sinners under Jesus' blood. Romans 8:1, reminds us that there is no condemnation in Christ Jesus!

God has been showing me this week that He has called me, He does love me, and His ways are so much higher than mine (Isaiah 55:8). I cannot even begin to delve into everything that has happened, but I don't think I've ever felt this close to the Father before. I find that every tissue and fiber within me is screaming, "Jesus, bid me come and die!" If any part of me revolts against that call, I pray that the Father would purify me and cleanse me from all my unrighteousness (1 John 1:9).

I have had the opportunity to go to a local reservoir three times in the past week. I cannot begin to explain the deep emotional healing I have felt taking place as a result of my frequent visits to the man-made body of water. Yes, I was extremely tired from getting out that much, but the Lord met me there.

Sunday night I went with a close friend whom I connect with on many levels. We sat there and listened to praise and worship music on her laptop, praising our Savior with hands lifted and hearts raised to heaven. I couldn't help but look at the beauty of His creation and not believe. I do not understand for the life of me how anyone can look at the sunset or even feel the wind and not believe!

The fact is, though, millions don't. Sadder still, millions think they know Jesus, but in reality they have no idea. Or maybe saddest yet, millions know the Savior but sit on their hands with the truth that would set their friends, their co-workers, their city free! Oh how greedy we've become. The gospel is not meant to be hoarded by the ones who are blessed to have found its freedom. Millions of people are dying and don't even know it. We sit around condemning people right and left, leaving the truth shut inside our doors for the Sunday-only Christians. I'm just as guilty as anyone of having preconceived notions about people or failing to show the grace that the Father has bestowed upon all of us who are found in Christ.

The immense beauty our Father has set before us is so God-breathed, so breathtaking. It's a good thing I had my oxygen with me. I couldn't help but get tears in my eyes looking at the sun setting over the water and the purplish pink clouds across the sky. I can't help but wonder if He's up in heaven saying, "Look!! I made that tree for you. See the leaves rustling in the wind? That's me. And if you think I made great trees, just think about you and the plans I have laid out for your life, if you'd just give Me the time of day!"

Why He does not strike us dead for our lack of awareness of His holiness, I will never understand. Although I have been hammering home grace lately, I cannot help but be alarmed at how cheap grace seems to be to some Christians. They wallow in a grace that treats God like a vending machine, thinking they can just ask for forgiveness because God knows they are going to sin anyway. How abominable can we get? God is holy and just, and He demands that He be given the glory He so rightfully deserves. If He didn't, He wouldn't be God. God cannot lie or break any promises. In His Word He clearly states that all the glory and honor is to go back to Him. The more we grasp that concept, the more we realize that even though we'll never succeed in giving Him the proper reverence that He deserves, it's our joy to try with all that we have, laying aside everything that hinders us along the way. May we not wallow in cheap grace and lose sight of the sheer awe that comes from knowing a transcendent God. He is alive and working among us.

It still is well...

SEPTEMBER 2005: SO TIRED...

- Fev1 anywhere from 16-20% using Columbus Children's scale[14]
- Oxygen turned up to 4.0 L but still couldn't breathe very well
- My favorite phrase, "I'm so tired."
- Strength was waning and was hardly able to leave the bedroom
- Sleep was hard to achieve and never restful, though I slept for hours a day
- Calls made to best friends scattered across the country, telling them how much I love them but that I long for them to love Jesus more
- By God's grace, spoke at a Saturday night prayer session for *Teens for Christ*
- Surgeon was out of the country from September 13-24, 2004
- Moved to inactive status on the United Network Organ Sharing national registry, not what I was expecting-at all

CHAPTER SEVEN

Desperation: Part Two

I said along with Paul: "To live is Christ, and to die is gain" (Phil. 1:21). I began focusing much more on the *second* half of that statement, as everything within me cried for more of Him even though my body was failing me, and my strength was almost gone. I made calls to friends spread across the nation, and in my heart, I've begun to plan to see my Savior face-to-face.

"Holiness is a state of soul in which all the powers of the body and mind are consciously given to God."

—Phoebe Palmer

September 1, 2005–Days #122-127:
Still alive
Days #122–127 on the list are over!

*E*very time something else happens, I just sit back and laugh and praise Him for not only putting up with me but using me in amazing, incredible ways. I can't minister to the people that others can. I can't live out another person's story. I don't even want to try. God made us all different for a reason. We are all ordinary, yet with God, we can do *extraordinary* things. The Holy Spirit within us gives us power, Christ *in* us, the hope of glory (Colossians 1:27). Our days *truly* are short; we don't know what tomorrow holds (Proverbs 27:1). James reminded us that we are "just a vapor that appears for a little while and then vanishes away" (James 4:14). What kind of legacy am I going to leave? This young woman may die at age twenty-two, but God is *still* Sovereign and still good.

I don't understand why some are called to live by a faith that doesn't seem to require much earthly sacrifice, while others are called to live out what some may call a "radical" faith. In the Bible, people gave their lives for the cause of Christ, and they did it willingly. They weren't asking for tax breaks or more blessings. They just wanted more of Him. Isn't that what we're here for, to glorify God in all that we do (1 Corinthians 10:31)? If we were going on what the flesh wants, I would have had my surgery a long time ago. To live is Christ, and to die is gain (Phil. 1:21).

In Philippians 3, we learn to say with Paul that we are forgetting what lies behind and are reaching forward to what lies ahead (v. 13b), pressing on to the upward call of God in Christ Jesus (v14). Where God goes is exactly where I want to be. He beckons, and I come. He breathes in, and I breathe out. I can't do anything without Him. The realization of that fact is becoming clearer and clearer to me with every passing moment.

Maybe I'm closer to the transplant than I can imagine. But at the same time, even if I'm not, I am getting so many opportunities to choose to bless His name (Job19:25-27). Even when my flesh is so weak, my spirit is so willing to press on. There are times when I just want to give up, when I get so overwhelmed by emotion that I think I'm going to drown. That's when Jesus comes in, wraps His arms around me, and reminds me that I am loved by the Creator of the universe! He knows the number of hairs on my head, and He promises that if I profess Him before men, He'll profess me before my Father in Heaven (Matthew 10:28-32).

So often I fail to let Him be the one to complete me and bring me joy. I find myself looking for completion and comfort in friends, in someone else's relationship with Christ instead of my own, in authors who know much more than I ever will, and sometimes even in my dreams of the future. I have to stand in the power of Christ now, not yesterday or tomorrow, but right now. He alone is the reason I'm still alive. If I thought about everything bad that has happened to me in the past year, I'd be a wreck. It's September, meaning it has been almost a year since I started my downward slide physically. I had a good three weeks at college (if that) before God seemed to pull all the stops and began pulling apart my life piece by piece. *Thank You, Father for doing so. You hold my hand every single moment of every single day, and even though I've never seen You, nobody can tell me You don't exist.*

Isaiah 66 1-2 says, "Thus says the LORD, 'Heaven is My throne and the earth is My footstool. Where then is a house you could build for Me? And where is a place that I may rest? For My hand made all these things, thus all these things came into being,' declares the LORD. 'But to this one I will look, to him who is humble and contrite of spirit, and who trembles at My word.'" It's when we're still, when we're humble, that He redeems us from the pit and crowns us with loving kindness and compassion (Psalm 103:4).

Today I felt like I had so many balls in the air at the same time, that at one point I was sure something was going to come crashing down on me. Columbus Children's called to tell me that my wonderful, highly-skilled surgeon will be out of the country from September 13-24. This all means that for eleven days, I will be inactive on the transplant waiting list, since there wouldn't be a surgeon to do the surgery if lungs were even to come up. If they were to become available, I'd have to turn them down and just wait longer, possibly months. Eleven days seems like an eternity to me. I live hour-by-hour. I've already waited 127 days and the thought of lungs possibly coming up during those critical 264 hours and not being able to do a thing about it didn't sit well with my parents. One more lung infection and I could very easily die. I'd be gone and at Home with my sweet Jesus. Saying, "If I die, I die," to my parents, though doesn't go over well. I mean they're my parents. So my surgeon ended up calling my folks tonight to explain to them that he's going to Argentina. He did say that if I got really, really bad while he was gone, he'd try to come home. So that's comforting. He and Dr. Astor have talked, though, and they think I'm stable enough for him to leave, considering he's had this trip planned for over a year.

The prospect of waiting some more doesn't really sit well with me. I can't say that I trusted the Lord the whole day with this situation. I was surprised that I was as calm as I was with the severity of the situation. Part of me really wanted to scream, "God, do You not see me dying down here? Do you even care?" Of course He cares. He knows, He's in control. If I have to wait until Christmas, I wait. If I go Home in the process, I go Home. That doesn't mean I don't matter to Him, that my desires don't mean a thing, or that the Lord is up in heaven plotting ways to kill me off just to get back at me for all the times I've failed to acknowledge His power in my life.

I have to keep holding on to Him, holding on to that hope that I have within me. I miss my friends dearly; I long for their hugs and the ability to just be in their presence, but I must remember that my completion is in Christ alone. I have two wonderful parents who both love the Lord. They've both grown tremendously through this whole ordeal, and I'm reminded even in my own home that it's not about just me and *my* faith—no, not at all.

SEPTEMBER 8, 2005–DAYS #128-134: BREAK ME DAYS #128–134 ON THE LIST ARE OVER!

I hold on to Jesus' words:

"But seek first His kingdom and His righteousness; and all these things will be added to you. So do not be anxious for tomorrow; for tomorrow will care for itself. Each day has enough trouble of its own" (Matthew 6:33-34). "Looking up, they saw that the stone had been rolled away, although it was extremely large. And entering the tomb, they saw a young man sitting at the right, wearing a white robe; and they were amazed. And he said to them, "Do not be amazed; you are looking for Jesus the Nazarene, who has been crucified. He has risen; He is not here; behold, here is the place where they laid Him. But go, tell His disciples and Peter, 'He is going before you into Galilee; there you will see Him, just as He said to you.'"

—Mark 16:4-7

Jesus is alive and well. The cross is not where he stayed. The resurrection doesn't seem to get the publicity it deserves. The tomb has been rolled away. We do indeed serve a risen Savior. In life or death, I am His. I love Him so much more than I ever thought possible, and I know I'm only beginning. If God can crush my pride, heal my wounds, and light a fire within me where only embers once flickered, I have *no* doubt in my mind He can do the same for anyone.

I leave you with a prayer:

Oh, Father God, You are so much more than we will ever fathom. You are Father, You are Creator, Sustainer–You are everything we could ever need, and more. Lord, we don't even understand Your holiness, but I am so thankful that You are a God of Your Word. You demand holiness because You're God and there is none other. Father, I'm so thankful that You call us out, that You drive us to our knees, that You love us with a love that is indescribable. Lord, I know that You've been calling me lately just to get flat on my face and pray, pray until I don't know what else to say.

Father, I know I haven't been praying as much as I should, but Lord, how I long to see You move. I want Your will more than anything in this world. But Lord, I'm so tired, please continue to either offer the grace to press on or move me on to another part of this journey. You've proven Yourself so faithful, Lord. You owe me nothing, yet You seem to give endlessly. When I don't think I have the strength to go one more day, You come through. You show me that it's not me to begin with, it's You. You keep the world spinning, and You keep me in the palm of Your hand, as well.

Oh, Father, You are my deepest joy. There is nothing on this earth that brings me more joy than bringing You glory, seeing You move in me and through me. Father, I want to apologize for any hint of pride that is in my life, because I know that I have an ongoing problem there that I'm combating with all that I have. But it still comes up. Lord, beat any part of me that is anything but You into submission. I want more of You. I don't want to be content with what I've learned over this past year. I want to know more. I want to see You as You are, to glimpse just a bit of Your glory.

Oh, Father, unveil my eyes, I want to love You, Jesus. I want others to come to know You the way I have. You're so pure, so holy, so righteous, yet so available to Your people. Thank you, Father, I don't need lungs, I don't need anything but You, Lord, You know my heart, the secrets that lie within, yet You love me still. I'll never understand it, but I can't help but be caught up in You, in what You're doing. May all my words be from You and to You, not for humans' praise. Whatever You want to do with me, make me content. Make me dig, make me crawl to You if you have to. Use me, break me, make me burn with passion and fire for You and You alone. I love You, Jesus. I love You, Father, and I love You, Spirit, the Three in One. In the name of my Healer, Redeemer, and Coming King. Amen.

SEPTEMBER 11, 2005–DAYS #135-137: WHO COULD ASK FOR ANYTHING MORE? DAYS #135, 136 & 137 ARE OVER!

"And He has said to me, 'My grace is sufficient for you, for power is perfected in weakness.' Most gladly, therefore, I will rather boast about my weaknesses, that the power of Christ may dwell in me."

—2 Corinthians 12:9

I have not been very good about coming out and thanking everyone for their prayers. But that doesn't mean I'm not appreciative. I realize that hundreds, possibly even thousands of people, are praying for me daily, and I cannot help but feel those prayers have been sustaining me the past few weeks. Many have so selflessly blessed me through their time of intercession on my behalf. I've never felt so small in my life, so small yet so powerful in Him.

These past 365 days I have learned what Paul meant when he said, "To live is Christ." Nothing could have ever prepared me for all the events and twists and turns that have occurred. But I wouldn't trade the life lessons I've learned for any amount of health. I would do it all again in a heartbeat, but I'm so thankful I don't have to. I will do anything He wants me to do, even give up my life; it's not mine to begin with, anyway. I'm not afraid to die for the One who set me free, but oh how I long to live for Him, to do so much in His name.

I become so afraid, though, to be a dreamer, to believe in the plans that I feel God Himself has laid upon my heart. Is it me? Is it God? Sometimes I just don't know, and there's nothing more in my life that bothers me than that. I pray that wherever He would lead me, I'd be more than willing to serve. There is this feeling I get that tells me He wants to use me in ways I could never imagine. I do not say this out of pride or arrogance. If He does want to do such things, nothing I can do is going to change that if I'm laying my life at His throne. But what if I'm not giving myself totally to His cause, then what? Doubts. Fears. All from Satan himself. That's not freedom. That's not life more abundant. That's not how I want to feel.

I'm just so burdened for so many people. I know I'm getting weaker by the day; this is not news to me or to my family. It's hard to put into words how I feel. Someone told me today that I've definitely mellowed over the past month. Not that I'm not the same person, and I do have my moments where I'm loud and crazy. But for the most part, I'm longing for three things: 1) My Jesus to hold me and tell me He's proud of me; 2) My family and friends to know beyond a shadow of a doubt that I love them and only want them to love Jesus more than anything; 3) To be loved and truly known by the ones I love the most.

An overall theme I've established this past month with my friends has been this: I love you, and long for you to love Jesus more than anything. Simple as that. Sure, I want them to love me, but if they forget me completely and love Jesus all the more, so be it. I just want what's best for them, no matter what that is. I know what it means to crawl to the Father with nothing in my hands. I still only need one thing, Christ. I don't even need lungs. Without Jesus, I have nothing. Without Christ, I am aimlessly wandering through life, living on temporal happiness.

I've been reading the Sermon on the Mount a lot recently. I guess I just connect to it, especially right now. Jesus' words mean so much more now that I'm dependent on Him for so much more. Jesus opens the sermon with the Beatitudes:

The Beatitudes: Matthew 5:3-12 (NASB)

Blessed are the poor in spirit, for theirs is the kingdom of heaven.

Blessed are those who mourn, for they shall be comforted.

Blessed are the gentle, for they shall inherit the earth.

Blessed are those who hunger and thirst for righteousness, for they shall be satisfied.

Blessed are the merciful, for they shall receive mercy.

Blessed are the pure in heart, for they shall see God.

Blessed are the peacemakers, for they shall be called sons of God.

Blessed are those who have been persecuted for the sake of righteousness, for theirs is the kingdom of heaven.

Blessed are you when people insult you and persecute you, and say all kinds of evil against you falsely on account of Me.

Rejoice, and be glad, for your reward in heaven is great, for so they persecuted the prophets who were before you.

God has been showing me, through my weakness, that I truly am blessed when I rely completely on the Lord, whether that be by being gentle, mourning, seeking righteousness, or being merciful. It's when I put the focus back on Him that I truly feel satisfied.

Life has become interestingly quiet and peaceful for me the past couple of days. I don't feel the need to prove anything to anyone. It's hard to explain. I know that I'm running my race with all that I have, and no matter what happens, I love Jesus more than anything. I'm so ready to trade this tired body for a healthier, vibrant one! My day is coming; I can feel it. Maybe it'll even be tomorrow.

SEPTEMBER 20, 2005 – DAYS #138-146: DISCERNMENT
DAYS #138–146 ON THE LIST ARE OVER...

"The Lord hath done great things for us; whereof we are glad."

—Psalm 126:3 (KJV)

Christ is sustaining me, giving me a hope and a joy that I will never be able to deny. I don't know what's next, but I know He's been faithful time and time again, so I'm not afraid. I keep telling my friends that next week they'll call me up and tell me I have cancer. Not funny, I know, but I can't help but wonder what they'll ask for next. All I know is this: Jesus still sits on the throne; God is still God. Psalm 73:26-28 rings true: "My flesh and my heart may fail, but God is the strength of my heart and my portion forever. For behold, those who are far from you will perish; You have destroyed all those who are unfaithful to You. I have made the Lord God my refuge, that I may tell of all Your works."

Looking back, I see that the Lord began His work in me before I went to Cedarville. By the time I got to Cedarville, He gave me a clear choice: Go here with me or don't. I've never felt God speak to me more clearly before in my life. I have a very hard time with people who say the Spirit doesn't speak anymore. They don't know my God. I did not hear an audible voice, but in a way it was clearer than it would have been if someone was standing right in front of me. I knew what I was supposed to do and, by the grace of God, I made the right decision. I thank the Lord every day for bringing someone into my life who was willing to call me out, to speak truth into my life when I didn't want to hear it, when the answers to her questions weren't easy. Because of Him using her, I will never be the same. Yes, I made the decision, but we must not forget that every breath we take, every movement we make is because He allows us. I don't understand how all the theology goes together, but I've also learned that saying "I don't know" is one of the most freeing things I'll ever do. When it all comes down to it, we don't know much of anything in the grand scheme of things. We think we do, but we have no idea.

God doesn't want part of us, or even ninety percent of us. He cannot use us to our full potential until we give Him 100 percent of every facet of our lives. I'm not saying that we'll somehow become perfect. I am far from perfect. I'm thankful though, that I have friends who have shown me how the body is supposed to work, who tell me things I don't want to hear.

God continues to show me that He loves me, and He has called me because He wants to use me, not because He is obligated to do so. I'm terrified to trust my own discernment and do what I feel He's called me to do. I guess I have to learn to trust myself, knowing that it is He at work through me. The Holy Spirit doesn't need me to convict someone, but if He wants to use me to speak to someone, who am I to say I won't do it? I can acknowledge my fear and pray against it, but I cannot let it hinder me from doing what God has called me to do. I know that it is true that pride will kill. But vulnerability will set us free.

I know that God is sovereign over all situations, and nothing that is going on is surprising to Him. He knew what we were going to do yesterday, He knows everything about tomorrow, and He knows the events that will lead up to our death. He is the Alpha and the Omega (Rev. 21:6), the beginning and the end. His transcendence, omnipotence, and omniscience make God so much more than our finite minds comprehend. 1 Corinthians 13:12: "For now we see in a mirror dimly, but then face to face; now I know in part, but then shall know fully just as I also have been fully known."

CHAPTER EIGHT

Stillness

SEPTEMBER 24–25, 2005

"I am no longer anxious about anything, as I realize that He is able to carry out His will for me. It does not matter where He places me, or how. That is for Him to consider, not me, for in the easiest positions He will give me grace, and in the most difficult ones, His grace will be sufficient."

—Hudson Taylor

AND THEN IN AN INSTANT…

LIFE CHANGED FOREVER.

SEPTEMBER 24, 2005
THE UN-EDITED EMAIL FROM ALLIE AROUND 6:00 P.M.

*H*ey everyone it's allie but I have some incredible news! Amber just received the call and she is on her way to

Columbus for her lungs! She doesn't have time to inform you all, I'm sorry. She needs to leave RIGHT now. Pray hard! She'll contact you as soon as she can.

Love you all very much! Amber sends her love.

God bless, allie

Reflections

Allie:

I have been friends with Amber for several years now. We grew very close to each other in high school. Throughout the years we have shared many laughs and tears together. I have always known Amber to be very strong and courageous. She has been through so much and she has battled cystic fibrosis for so long, yet she continues to follow God and put other people first.

During our freshman year of college, Amber's health became tremendously worse. After moving back home, she continued to love God and search deeper into His Word. Meanwhile, I was at school in Mount Vernon. Because I hadn't seen Amber in weeks, I came home for the weekend so that I could spend some time with her. I brought along two of my friends and we spent a few hours on Friday night with Amber. We went back Saturday evening to spend some more time with her as well. We hadn't been there five minutes when Amber received the call from Columbus that they had a lung donor for her. The news was incredibly exciting and it threw us all into a state of panic and no one could think straight because they needed to leave for Columbus right then. Amber needed to pack an overnight bag and my friends helped her with that while I tried desperately to send out an email to all of Amber's friends.

Meanwhile, Amber's parents were making all the arrangements and gathering everything they needed. After Amber and her family had left for Columbus, my friends and I went to pick her sister up at a campground, and then we took her to her grandparent's house. Later that night, after Amber received word that the lungs were good and that they were going to go ahead with the transplant, my friends and I drove down to the Columbus Children's Hospital where we waited all night for her to come out of surgery. During this time, my friends were incredible in comforting me and calming me down as I waited to hear that Amber was out of surgery and doing well.

Amber did wonderfully in surgery, and I truly believe that God was with the surgeons and at work the entire time. Since the surgery, Amber has done very well and continues to get stronger. She is an amazing young woman who loves God dearly. She is currently sharing her story with many others across the nation and sharing with them all that God has done in her life. Amber has been a great encouragement to me and many others. She inspires us all.

Heather

It was my first year teaching at Wapakoneta High School, and it was third period one day when some students filed into my classroom eager to learn the world of chemistry. There was one girl who stuck out. She stuck out because she was so energetic and full of life. She also stuck out because she coughed a lot. At the time, I had no experience with cystic fibrosis. All I knew was that people with cystic fibrosis had terrible coughs and also died at a young age. I noticed that none of the students were affected by Amber's coughing, indicating to me that they were used to this. After a few days of school, I remember thinking that she must have an illness, and I hoped that it wasn't cystic fibrosis. A couple days later, I received in my mailbox medical alerts for all of my students who had health issues. As I flipped through the papers, I came across Amber's sheet. My heart sank as I read the culprit of her coughing–cystic fibrosis. How terrible, I thought, because in the two weeks that I knew her, she seemed to be such a nice girl, so positive and lively. I couldn't help but think that she was reaching the life expectancy for someone with this disease. I quickly learned that the disease wasn't Amber's identity.

Looking back, I don't remember how Amber and I became close. I remember how passionate Amber was about learning and how she constantly pushed herself. I was in awe of her because I felt that if I was in her position, I don't think that I would have been in school. I'd be enjoying my last years by traveling and vacationing in warm locations. That is what makes Amber so much better than me. Amber doesn't live to die. She lives to get the most out of each day and to make a difference each day.

Every winter, Amber found herself in the hospital for an intense round of antibiotics to try and fight what the weather was doing to her body. Inevitably, the hospital stays usually caused Amber to miss some school. Weeks later, when Amber returned to school, she insisted on completing all of her missed assignments in all of her classes, regardless of how overwhelming it was for her. She didn't want to miss out on any knowledge that she could acquire.

I remember Amber standing with me in my classroom and she was understandably feeling overwhelmed with life. She was explaining how she felt her disease was alienating her from her friends. I didn't know what to say to comfort her. What words were worthy enough to try and solace her? I couldn't tell her that everything was okay because it wasn't. She was not okay. This horrific disease was claiming her body while her spirit fought to go on. I realized that there wasn't anything I could say. I simply needed to listen to her. I knew she would come to a resolution and she would continue the fight for her life.

Amber's faith is so strong, and since I grew up in a non-religious home, I was always intimidated by her intense devotion to God. How could she be so dedicated to someone who dealt her such a rotten hand? I even doubted His existence because if there was a God, why would He let such atrocities occur on Earth and why would He create such a wonderful person in Amber only to take her from us prematurely?

My thoughts all changed on Saturday, September 24th. It seemed like a regular day. Nothing special was happening at my house until that afternoon when the phone rang. It was Lindsey Short, a friend of Amber's and also a former student of mine. I knew that when I received a phone call from her, Amber was enroute to Columbus for her transplant. My heart was racing with excitement for Amber as Lindsey told me the anticipated news. "It's time," Lindsey said. "She's on her way." Lindsey and I made arrangements for me to pick her up at college that evening and travel to Columbus to await the results of Amber's transplant. After I hung up the phone with Lindsey, I cried and prayed that Amber would make it through the surgery. She had to. There was so much more she had to do with her life. She had to spread His Word and He certainly wouldn't take her and prevent her from doing this.

I picked up Lindsey from college that evening and we set out for Columbus. The car ride passed quickly as we shared our favorite stories of Amber and cranked up the volume to songs on the radio that reminded us of her. Before we knew it, we were at the hospital. We made our way to the surgery waiting room and found it full of Amber's family and friends.

I immediately felt out of place as I soon realized I was the least religious person there. How selfish I felt for wanting to be there when a much more religious person could have taken my place—someone who had a relationship with God, perhaps someone whose prayers for Amber had a better chance of being answered. Why would He listen to my prayers when I had done nothing to serve Him?

Amber's family and friends welcomed Lindsey and me with open arms and told us that she had just been taken into surgery. The time was midnight and Amber had just begun a ten-to-twelve-hour surgery. The group of us played some Yahtzee and prayed, anxiously awaiting any word on the progress of the surgery. I remember falling asleep from 5:30 A.M. to 7:30 A.M. as we were still waiting for news about the surgery. By 10:30 A.M., the doctors reported that the double lung transplant was a success and that they were closing Amber up and would be out in about an hour to discuss the procedure with her parents.

I immediately began to cry upon hearing that everything went well. I noticed I was the only one who cried, probably because I was the one who trusted God the least. Everyone else put their faith in Him and knew that He would do what was best. In retrospect, at some point in those early hours I remember thinking that if God does exist and is indeed as good as all of these people believe, then Amber should survive the surgery. As the morning progressed, it felt almost as if He was in the waiting room with us, listening to our prayers and calming our fears. From the moment that we received the good news, I knew that God does exist and that He is truly wonderful. There is no other way to explain why Amber's surgery went as well as it did. It was perfect, and I know that we have Him to praise for it.

As teachers, we want the best for our students. We want them to succeed, to find happiness and love, and to do something with their lives that they are passionate about. I wished all of this for Amber and she, of course, achieved it. There are still so many more lives Amber has yet to touch and I suppose we will share her with the rest of the country as her faith and triumph have earned her fame!

So the lesson I learned from Amber is to not live like you are dying. Live every day to the fullest, make a difference in someone's life, love unselfishly, be passionate, and put your faith in God and your life will be complete.

Allison:

> [For I always pray to] the God of our Lord Jesus Christ, the Father of glory, that He may grant you a spirit of wisdom and revelation [of insight into mysteries and secrets] in the [deep and intimate] knowledge of Him…
>
> —Ephesians 1:17 (AMP)

This is the prayer that has been prayed for us for a long time—centuries, actually—the prayer that all of us would know God deeply and intimately in every way that He can be known. "Eternal life is to know Me," Jesus says.

Since the time I began following Jesus, I've looked back at my life and I am very surprised and sometimes rather confused about what I have been a part of and seen, the people that I know, how I know them, etc. It all seems rather strange to me, a mystery to give it a word. In the midst of a mystery embodying my life I see a plan. It is a very strategic well-thought-out plan, that what I have been a part of, and seen and heard, the places I have gone, the people I have encountered and know, could not have occurred unless someone had sat down and figured out how all of it was going to happen. In other words, someone had to have planned all of this. And I am discovering as I continue to live that when we give God the script of our lives for Him and Him alone to write, we will find our lives being a mystery, even to ourselves.

My friendship and relationship with Amber is a part of that mystery that I can only respond to with adoration toward God. His hand that is so near and so personal leaves me with no words, no thoughts, and no great ideas, but only an incredibly deep response of awe and adoration of Who He is.

I attend The Ohio State University where I am a senior. I am one of many people who help with a campus-wide House of Prayer that God has been planning and leading for quite some time. The House of Prayer is a network of different churches and ministries on campus to cover the university in nonstop 24/7 prayer. All prayer happens at a central location. It is a house where no one lives but Jesus, where students and leaders from all over the OSU campus and Columbus area come and pray engaging with Him in all kinds of creative ways. There is a website for the House of Prayer, as well as a blog where we post crazy God stuff. Our blog is made up of a network of blogs from all over the world, one of which belongs to an Amber N. Metz. During one of Amber's many late nights, she "stumbled" across our blog for the prayer house at OSU and wrote me an encouraging email. Her email rocked my world and I wrote her back to tell her thanks for the encouragement. It was cool to see that she was from Ohio, etc. This began a long series of emails back and forth between Amber and me.

God used Amber's story to draw my heart nearer to His. I found myself being deeply amazed and inspired by Amber. I enjoyed and fell in love with her as she shared her life with me via email. The passionate love of Jesus and the goodness of God were speaking loud and clear to me through her. She had given the script of her life to God to write as He will, and her life was being wrapped up in a mystery. Almost everything about this young woman did not make any sense, yet it all made perfect sense because she knew Jesus. She was on a breathing machine, in very poor physical condition, stuck in a bed. In fact, she had a funeral planned. But she was passionately in love with her King, on fire for her King, bold for her King, and preaching to everyone she could from where she was (in a small bedroom in Wapakoneta, Ohio) about Jesus the King and His Kingdom.

Right after a mass email Amber had sent out on September 1, 2005 with the subject line "Still Alive," she sent me a personal email where she wrote: "It may sound crazy, but I think the Lord's calling me to get well and take off. I don't know how, but He does." It was at this point that I began to really believe this too, that God did not have plans for Amber to go Home anytime soon, but somehow this young woman who has lived past the time the doctors said she would live was going to breathe again and tell her story. That story is a testimony of Life.

Amber's double lung transplant "happened" to be in Columbus where I was living, five minutes from my house. Our first meeting was a week or so after her surgery when I was the first to kidnap her (not really) from the hospital. It was her first time being out after her surgery, and I was honored to be so near in vicinity to her. I took her to the OSU campus for some real food (non-hospital food) and a tour of the House of Prayer on campus where we also spent a glorious hour of prayer together. I realized in this first physical encounter with one another that I really had never met anyone quite the same as me "My long-lost twin" we kept saying in reference to each other.

I snagged Amber one last time before she headed home to Wapakoneta for some more grub and conversation, as well as another visit to the House of Prayer during one of our twenty-four- hour prayer vigils. At the prayer vigil, I thoroughly enjoyed seeing the reactions people had when Amber told them she had just undergone a double lung transplant. Then they heard her pray to God with passion, power, and boldness, and their reactions went to shock—"Who is this woman?" As I stood at the side of the room, I was also amazed at how a person could have such a booming voice and move around as she did after such a surgery. I am still amazed. I am still standing with the shocked people where I respond in adoration to this great God.

Included in the Bible in an incredible revelation that John received on the island of Patmos many years ago that he was instructed to write down for us. John heard a voice shouting across the heavens that the people of God have conquered Satan by the means of the blood of the Lamb and by the very word of their testimony. There is also something very interesting in 2 Corinthians 10:4 that Paul, the writer, reminds us of. We are told that the people of God do not wage war as the world does with physical weapons, weapons of flesh and blood, but that the weapons of God's people are weapons mighty before Him for the destruction and the overthrow of Satan's strongholds. I am convinced that these words from Scripture are true and that Amber's testimony will by God and for God accomplish more than we could imagine possible.

Christ Jesus, I pray for Your Kingdom to come and Your perfect will to be done in every reader of this book. Invade our lives with Your reality, God.

With much love and prayer,
Allison Brooks
www.LoveOsu.com

Leanna:

I was acquainted with Amber through the ministry of *Teens for Christ* (TFC) and got to know her while we were on the TFC ministry team together. Before meeting Amber, I vaguely knew about cystic fibrosis but had never known anyone who had it. I really got close to Amber after she left Cedarville University and came home in the winter of 2005. She started discipling me, which is what Amber and I called "doing life together." We shared Scripture with one another, told each other what God was showing us in our personal lives, prayed together, and just talked about the awesome and mighty God we serve.

A few weeks after Amber came home, her health declined so severely that she was unable to drive. So I would drive over to her house at least once a week to be able to meet with her. After the summer months passed she was going downhill very fast. It was hard watching Amber struggling to breathe. At the same time it was so wonderful to see someone so much submitted to God. She just glowed. She was so content. She clung to the words Paul wrote in Philippians 1:21, "For to me, to live is Christ, and to die is gain."

I remember when the call arrived that she had lungs. I was with the ministry team at the *Teens for Christ* Kick-Off. Immediately people from all over were praying. I was so fortunate to be able to go to the hospital with Buck and Kristin after the Kick-Off. We made it just in time to hug her and pray with her right before they wheeled her into the operating room. If I hadn't been with Buck and Kristin I might not have been able to see her. But because Buck was clergy, I got in. Right before surgery, Amber, though very weak and sick, was full of energy and light.

The eleven hours of waiting during surgery were spent mainly in prayer. Though her parents were, of course, concerned, there was a peace that rested over the entire waiting room. The fervency and expectancy that God tells us to use when we pray to Him was being used, and God was there. After getting little sleep and with all the waiting, to hear that she did extremely well and that the lungs were perfect sent rejoicing throughout our group.

To see Amber now, you would not be able to tell that she had almost died. She is the most vibrant and full of life, driven and goal oriented person I know. God has certainly used her life to impact many, many people for His kingdom thus far! No doubt He is going to continue to glorify Himself through His willing servant Amber.

CHAPTER NINE

Beauty from Pain

The end of a reasonable creature is to attain beatitude, and that can only consist in the kingdom of God, which in turn is nothing else than the well-ordered society of those who enjoy the vision of God.

—St. Thomas Aquinas, (1225-1274)

OCTOBER 12, 2005–BREATHTAKING DAY #17 OUT OF SURGERY!

Author's Note: After asking a close friend (Ashley Whited) to get into my e-mail account, an e-mail was written just days after my surgery updating everyone on my progress. I did not compose a mass email, however, until I wrote the following from the Ronald McDonald House across the street from the hospital on October 12, 2005.

I know you all have been anxiously awaiting the details of what occurred in the past seventeen days. So, settle in, and allow me to take you back through the past seventeen days of my life. It's going to be a *breathtaking* experience!

We have to go back to Saturday, September 24th, to pick up where we left off. It's so odd for me, even though it has been only seventeen days, to try to get myself back in the mindset of how I used to feel. I do remember feeling pretty tired and run-down on that day, but for some reason I'm thinking it was even more than usual. In any case, the day started out like all the others did, not before 2:00 P.M. and with me on my computer, listening to music and hammering out emails.

The night before, Allie and her friends (Abbie & Andrew) from Mount Vernon Nazarene University came over, and we were randomly discussing how crazy it would be if I got "*The Call*" while they were at my house. Obviously, on Friday that didn't happen, but Saturday—that's a different story!

They were planning on stopping back over just for a few minutes on Saturday night before they went to the movies. Around 5:30 P.M., they showed up, and within twenty minutes my phone started ringing. I looked at the number and *knew* right away that it was Dr. Astor. He said the donor looked *extremely* promising, and I was to get to Columbus ASAP. I'll never forget the look on Allie's face—priceless! Let's just say they didn't make it to their movie!

In fact, Allie was put to work right away, writing one of my emails, driving to a campground to pick up my sister, driving her back to my grandma's, and then driving to Columbus to sit in the waiting room for twelve-plus hours. Just having that special memory with her means so much to both of us, and I have to thank Abbie and Andrew for not only coming to my house but for also spending the entire night at Columbus Children's on a hard floor. Neither one had known me more than twenty-four hours, yet they sacrificed their time and energy to come wait in the waiting room with the rest of my entourage.

We left my house with Allie and the crew still inside. My parents and I sped off to Columbus. The whole way there I talked on my phone! I don't remember how many phone calls I made and received during the duration of the trip, but the calls didn't end there. I was on my phone practically up until they took me into surgery at 11:30 P.M.

In any case, once I got to the hospital things moved rather quickly. It took around three hours to get everything set up, from meeting with Dr. Astor, to anesthesia to blood work, to x-ray, to hobnobbing with nurses and my pastor.

I think it was around 9:00 P.M. when Dr. Astor came in and said everything was a GO. At that moment, I honestly wasn't afraid. The "peace of God that passes all understanding" (Phil. 4:7) definitely was upon me and my family. I found it funny when my pastor went to pray with me, because I said I'd pray for myself, too. He said that I was the first patient in thirty-five years of ministry to pray for *herself* before their surgery. Praying surely didn't seem like such an oddity to me at that point!

For the next few hours, I continued talking on my phone (surprise, surprise), updating all my friends scattered around the country. Those calls were not easy to make, let me tell you. Literally five minutes before they took me back for surgery at 11:30 P.M., I got to see some of my closest friends one last time. To the following people, *thank you* for driving down to Columbus that clear Saturday night and waiting in the OR waiting room: My parents (Kent & Mary Ann), Abbie Bryer, Allison Reese, Andrew Bontrager, Gary Hohman, Amy Marshall, Buck & Kristin Sutton, Carla Brenneman, Garret Schymanski, Heather Harmon, Jesse Jordan, Leanna Teodosio, and Lindsey Short. To the rest of you who have visited, sent cards, gifts and *plenty* of prayers, I cannot begin to express how extremely loved and blessed I have felt over the course of the past seventeen days. All my love to *each* and every one of you.

After saying goodbye, they wheeled me through the double doors. Now, I had been talking about how this moment was going to feel for a *very* long time, but the emotions and thoughts that were running through my head that moment seemed to all point back to the Father, the One who set me free during this journey. I remember making sure that I had my CD with me (Passion '05), and after receiving my epidural and strawberry-flavored anesthesia I was ready to go. The last song I remember hearing was "How Great Is our God" by Chris Tomlin-how appropriate for the occasion!

Fast-forward to 11:00 A.M. Sunday morning, and my surgery was completed. The preparation for the surgery took around ninety minutes, followed by the actual procedure, which took around ten hours. I wasn't in the waiting room, obviously, but I hear that things went rather well. From praying to playing Yahtzee at 5:00 A.M., they all kept pretty busy—I guess as busy as anyone can when waiting to hear how a daughter/best friend is doing during her double lung transplant.

I woke up in ICU around 1:30 P.M. Yes, make all the jokes you want, but you can't keep me down for long! I'm told that twenty minutes after arriving in ICU, I gave a nurse a high-five. I remember seeing my parents, and my daddy was using Carla's camera to take video/digital pictures of me right after surgery. I'm told I also asked Dr. Astor to rub my feet, give me Mountain Dew and a Bible. A chaplain came and prayed with me…at least I think he did. I also remember seeing my parents, followed by my sister, my grandma, and my friend Mandy.

The next morning I got the tube out of my throat and was taken off of oxygen completely. Two days out of my surgery, I was sitting in a chair for eight hours. Carla and Mandy came back on Tuesday, and by Tuesday night I was out of ICU and on my way to 6W –the best nurses' station at Columbus Children's.

Now, consider this: I had been pretty much in the dark for more than two days, and they tried to move me at 10:00 o'clock at night, with bright florescent lights everywhere. I have a tendency to get migraines at times, and with all the narcotics I was on, I was already feeling one coming on. So after that traumatic move, I wanted to die. I remember Tuesday night lying in my bed, breathing just fine but in so much pain from my migraine that I was asking the Lord to just take me Home anyway. I didn't receive any relief until the next morning when they finally gave me Mountain Dew and some Benedryl. The migraine subsided, but I was unable to have any lights on or read for about six days or so. I had this running joke that I was going to shout "Praise God! I can breathe, but now I can't see." I slept in sunglasses, put blankets over the doors and windows, and pretty much hibernated. I had the Word read to me for a good ten days before I was able to dive into it myself.

As each day went by, more tubes were removed, and by Friday, Oct. 1, I was up on my feet (only five days out of my surgery). I never thought so many tubes and wires could fit on such a small person, but at least they're all gone now. All I had left was my port access, which is a far cry from where I was before.

I just cannot say thank you enough to the people in my life who have stuck by me through thick and thin. Even though a lot of them were not able to be in Columbus with me that night, I could never convey how much you mean to me or repay them for their love and support as my brothers and sisters in Christ.

I was prepared to go Home and meet the Lord, but now, looking back, I can say without a shadow of a doubt that it is only by the power of God that I am standing (and sitting, laughing, talking) here today! Praise be to Him and Him alone. Many of my friends and family have not had the chance to see me as of yet, so I am so excited to show them how well I am doing.

I cannot go any further without thanking Dr. Astor, Dr. Galantowicz, Dr. Phillips and every other person who was involved during my surgery. The Lord has blessed them with tremendous knowledge and expertise, and I feel very privileged to be under their care!

On Saturday, October 8th, after only thirteen days, I moved out of Columbus Children's and to the Ronald McDonald House across the street. Since then, I've been putting in about eighteen-to-twenty-hour days, doing IVs, therapy, doctor appointments, taking lots of pills, and pretty much just glorifying my Father with *every* breath I have. Soon I should be off most of my IVs and the aerosol treatments I've taken since I was a baby. As far as going home to Wapakoneta, I should bust out of here sometime in November.

I prayed about the emails I'd been writing for the past six months being turned into a book. I think I can now safely say that, Lord-willing, this will happen. *Breathtaking,* the title of the supposed book, seems to be less of a dream and more of a reality with every passing day. I am so excited! I want the Lord to use me in amazing, mighty, unpredictable ways.

That's my life in a nutshell. I'm almost to the point where I can get down on my face and praise Him. Who cares if I have so many stitches left? I cannot contain my joy, excitement, and utter awe of my Savior and Healer, Jesus Christ. He is the sole reason I live; there's no point in writing, singing, or dancing without Christ. The world will lie to us, Satan will deceive us, but Christ will set us free. To live is Christ and to die is gain. For the first time in a long time, I am focusing on the first part of that statement. Freedom is mine.

OCTOBER 25, 2005–HOME SWEET HOME
I'M HOME AFTER ONLY 29 DAYS

I am HOME! I'm excited to be back amongst the cornfields of northwestern Ohio. City life is definitely not for me, at least not for a very long time. I want to be where I can see for miles, look at the stars, and go to sleep in peace without sirens going off every ten minutes. I wasn't supposed to come home until sometime in November, but it looks as though the Lord had other plans.

I cannot begin to explain how truly miraculous my recovery has been. Hardly anyone believes that I'm only a month out of surgery. I'm up to twenty-five minutes of cardio workout without any problems. If I had been put on a treadmill/bike/stepper thirty days ago, I think I would have died. I also have recreational therapy two times a week, which involves muscle strengthening and stretching.

Everything is different now! Yesterday I had my first set of spirometry numbers taken (basically it measures my lung capacity). Twenty-nine days ago, I was sitting around 16% (+- 2) FEV1, but as of yesterday, I am sitting at 82%! That does not usually happen this early on! I'm only a month out, and I'm not far away from being at a normal range! I haven't seen 82% since I was probably ten years old. I have no words to say anymore! God is moving, and I can't wait to see what He has in store for me, for my family, for everyone!

I know God has placed exactly the right people in my life, and I'm eager to see what He does with all of us. Distance will never sever the friendships He has given to me—of this I'm sure. While I tell my parents all the time that I can't wait to get out of the house, I do thank the Lord every single day for my mom and dad. It thrills my soul to see them happy again. Not that they didn't trust the Lord during the whole process, but it certainly was a trying time for my family.

I will, Lord willing, one day get out of this house and out on my own, to do only God knows what. I'm okay with not knowing right now exactly what is going to take place. I can look into the future much more so than I could before. But at the same time,

I must be careful to take it a day at a time, knowing that my life is still but a vapor (James 4:14).

I am just in awe of our Lord's power in my life. Yes, I was faithful until the bitter end, but it is only by His grace that I had the strength to do so. Looking back, I honestly don't know how I made it, especially toward the end. I've had close friends tell me they used to lie to me and tell me I still looked good when in reality they were worried out of their minds. Things were not good from about August on, but now here we are at almost November; look how times have changed.

I'm looking out my window at my tree. My tree and I have a special bond. Last winter I used to stare out the window and wonder just how long it was going to take for new life to spring up on the tree and within me. I saw the leaves come back last spring, but my condition, at least physically, only got worse. As the trees flourished during the summer, there were times I found myself longing to be the tree, to feel full of life again, even though I knew the Lord was being glorified through my illness. As summer ended and my friends returned to college, the bottom seemed to fall out. The leaves were still on the trees, but I found myself feeling as if I was falling into the unknown. I was ready to go Home, to finally fall into the arms of my Savior.

September 24th came, though, and life hasn't been the same since. I'll never forget the events that led up to my chains being broken and my body being set free. My heart was set free a long time ago, but I'm well on my way to being able to say my spirit is willing and my flesh isn't so weak, at least in a physical sense.

I am still asking the Lord every day what exactly He's choosing me for on this amazing journey. The ones who know me best know how dumb I feel at times, how emotions can overwhelm me so easily, how prideful and closed I can become. The Lord knows, too, and He still wants me. More importantly, He still wants all of us—your flaws and all. There is no time like the *present* to come into His presence. We don't have to worry about cleaning out the sin in our lives first or reprioritizing our commitments. We come to the fountain and lay ourselves at the feet of the One who came to set us free (Isaiah 61.1).

> "Call to Me, and I will answer you, and I will tell you great and mighty things, which you do not know."
>
> —Jeremiah 33:3

I can attest to that statement. The Lord cannot go against His Word. If He could, what would be the point of serving such a fickle, self-centered God? No, He loves us. He wants us, but we must have willing hearts.

In Matthew 8, we see Jesus coming down from the mountain after giving the Sermon on the Mount to find a leper bowing down before Him. The leper said, "Lord, if You are willing, You can make me clean." Jesus stretched out His hand and touched him, saying, "I am willing; be cleansed." And immediately his leprosy was cleansed (Matthew 8:1-3). Jesus is more than willing to meet us where we are, but we must trust in Him enough to say with confidence, "You, Father, can do what You say You can do." May we continue to bow humbly at His feet, forsaking everything that hinders us from walking in His Truth, loving the lost instead of ostracizing them, and allowing the Holy Spirit to convict us where conviction is due. I never remember Jesus putting Himself higher than even the prostitutes. The more I read the Word, the less I see of the Jesus we, as Americans, tend to gravitate toward.

It seems to me that Jesus spoke the truth to everyone. He didn't shy away from His mission in life: to proclaim freedom through Himself. At the same time, He didn't jam the truth down the lost souls' throats. He had compassion on them, grieving for their souls. Even at the cross He said, "Forgive them, Father, for they know not what they do" (Luke 23:34). This doesn't sound like some power-hungry prophet to me.

We are called to walk in the light as He is in the light (1 John 1:7), not to classify people by their status. We must love God's children, knowing that it is only by His grace that we know Him ourselves. We cannot save anyone; we can only plant seeds and pray that someone else comes along to water the seed along the way. We've lost appreciation for the journey, wanting to hastily go from point A to point B in 0.5 seconds. There is a process that leads up to one's salvation; revelation that leads to salvation must begin somewhere. We don't end up kneeling at the cross without the Lord using someone or something to speak to us. Even if the process occurs quickly, it still occurs. Sanctification, too, is a life-long process that seems to have been lost among the programs and hoopla that occurs in some churches today. *Oh, Father, when will we get back to the basics of life and say with Paul, "To live is Christ, and to die is Gain"* (Phil. 1:21)?

On the other hand, Jesus did have choice words to say to the religious people of the time. Once we make Christianity a religion and not a relationship we've lost the whole point of knowing Jesus Christ. He didn't come to establish some world religion, He didn't come so that we Christians could lock the truth in churches with members who do nothing but complain about how they aren't getting anything out of what they're hearing. *Oh, Father, forgive us!* Jesus wants our hearts. I don't think He even cares about how much money we put in the offering plate if we aren't offering up our lives as an offering to Him every single day.

Father, may I humble myself in Your presence every single moment you give me. I breathe for You and You alone. My heart is overwhelmed at the beauty of Your ways. Here now I stand, saying I'm forever Yours. Jesus, You're my only Lord, and I will sing Your praise.

Reflections

Ashley:

There are three main lessons I've learned this year from knowing God, knowing Amber, and living life.

1. Joy is not circumstantial.

Joy is defined by www.dictionary.com as "the emotion of great delight or happiness caused by something exceptionally good or satisfying." I watched Amber for two years as her disease worsened, her lung capacity dwindled, and she struggled for every breath she took. Amber took it day-by-day, rested in God, and rejoiced in Him always. I remember spending a few nights at the local reservoir with Amber watching the sunset and singing praise songs to the Lord. Even in her weakest moments she still had so much joy that it overflowed out of her in worship and in life. Though she could barely breathe, she delighted in the Lord because He is "exceptionally good." How could a person so sick love God so much? Shouldn't she have been angry at Him for putting her through so much? No. Because God is sovereign. He does whatever it takes to make us like His Son.

2. God is above all.

Amber was in desperate need of a transplant. She was literally on her death bed. It was there that she truly found life in the Scriptures she read while lying there. Matthew 10:29-31 says that not one sparrow will fall apart from the Father, that we are more precious than any sparrow—even to the point that He has each hair on our heads numbered. It says that not one will fall apart from God. But still, the sparrows fall. God allows it to happen, just as He allowed Amber to have this disease and just as He chose to heal her.

Some would look at Amber's cystic fibrosis and question God's sovereignty. I do not. I look at Amber and her circumstances and I see a God who changes lives, who brings healing, who draws us to Himself no matter what it takes, and who uses our stories to tell the world that we have a Redeemer who lives. What if Amber never had cystic fibrosis? Would she be out speaking in churches, telling people that time is precious and should not be wasted? Would she value life differently? The point is, God allows life to happen to us so that we will take the stories He has given us and use those life lessons to tell the world about His Son, Jesus Christ.

3. Everyone has a story. Your faith counts!

We don't have to have a double lung transplant to have a valuable testimony. The book of John shows us how many people came to believe in Jesus through the testimonies of others. A testimony is simply our story. It's the journey God has taken us on. It's the life lessons He has taught you. It's the chiseling and purifying by fire He has done in our lives. In March 2006, my Dad was diagnosed with terminal cancer. I was devastated. But I turned to God and Scripture and was filled with joy, because joy is not circumstantial. I read a passage in Mark 2 that speaks of a paralyzed man being carried to Jesus by four of his friends. There were crowds surrounding Jesus so thickly that the four couldn't even get their friend to Him, except by going through the roof. So they went through the roof. The text says that when Jesus saw *their* faith, he turned to the paralyzed man and said, "Son, your sins are forgiven." I immediately noticed that the Word says that Jesus saw their faith, and as a result, the man was spiritually healed. He was forgiven. However, as far as most of those people were concerned, it wasn't spiritual healing that the man needed. The Pharisees even went as far as accusing Jesus of claiming to be God when He wasn't. Little did they know how wrong they were. They said to Jesus, "Who are You to forgive this man his sins? Only God can do that!" So Jesus asked them, would it be easier to announce the man's sins forgiven or to tell him to get up and walk? Obviously it would be easier to announce forgiveness because the results couldn't be seen. So to prove that He had the authority to do both, Jesus told the man to get up and walk. The paralyzed man immediately picked up his bed and left. People were glorifying God because of what they had seen!

When I read this passage I saw myself as one of those four men carrying my dad to Jesus. I wanted to see him physically healed, but even more than that, I wanted to see him spiritually healed. Dad and I have had some really good conversations the last few months about the Lord and where he will be spending eternity. He is spiritually healed. I do not take the glory, for it is God alone who saves. However, I do not deny the fact that my story, my faith, played a role in Dad's life. My family has spent the last few nights at the hospital with my dad. His kidneys are slowly failing and the doctors have stopped treatment for his cancer. He is here at home now, and is living the last of his days as comfortably as possible. While I did not see the physical healing of my dad, I saw a miracle nonetheless. And I saw God use me in my family in ways I never would have imagined. We all have a story. It may not be like Amber's, and it may not be like mine, but we all have a story to share with the world. We shouldn't be afraid to tell it.

In the past few years I've seen God work miracles in and through Amber and it has been an encouragement to me. I am thankful for her story and the impact it has had on my life. I know that joy is not circumstantial. I know that God is sovereign and I know that our faith, because of Jesus Christ, can change lives.

Author's Note:

I attended Ashley's father's funeral on September 10, 2006. He passed away on September 7, 2006 after an almost six month battle with kidney cancer.

NOVEMBER 11, 2005–LETTING GO
47 DAYS OUT OF SURGERY!

The Lord has given me *so* much to be thankful for, and I am still constantly amazed at the abilities and blessings He has showered upon me the past month-and-a half. Words come few and far between sometimes, but He knows my heart. It would take me a very long time to go into detail about what has been going on since I came home almost twenty days ago. But here's an update on how I'm doing physically: Therapy at Columbus Children's was completed on November 2nd (four-week program), and my bronchostomy (they take biopsies of your lungs to make sure there is no sign of rejection) on the 7th went very well. I've been working-out at least three times a week here at home, as well as trying to stay away from anyone who's sick.

Just the opportunity to go back down to Cedarville to visit exhilarates me. Cedarville's where I learned to fly, where the Lord broke me in *all* ways and began putting me back together with His love. I have a feeling it's going to be somewhat emotional going back and seeing the campus, sitting by the lake where I used to have long talks with God. I love the people, the atmosphere, and most of all, the memories. *Thank you, Father, for killing me and filling me with You. I know that I would not be the person I am today if You had not allowed me to go through the journey I have, not just physically but emotionally-speaking, as well.*

I am *passionate* about Truth, as you all know. I'm not about to shy away from the Word of God and the commands and promises inside. At the same time, I've learned that once I have done what the Lord has called me to do, there is nothing left to say. Only each of us on our own can ask the Lord to break us and put us back together. I made the decision at Cedarville that night at the lake, and my life has never been the same. I do not understand how God's sovereignty and our wills work together, but I know the leper in Matthew 8 said, "If you are willing, You

181

can make me clean." The man demonstrated his faith by those words, and the Lord healed him. The leper, though, had to have faith that Jesus was who He said he was.

All the things I used to deny, to hide from, and to shove under the rug, I now embrace because of the power of the Cross. It's not so much about "What can I do for God?" as it is "What has God brought me through?" "And He has said to me, 'My grace is sufficient for you, for power is perfected in weakness.' Most gladly, therefore, I will rather boast about my weaknesses, that the power of Christ may dwell in me. Therefore I am well content with weaknesses, with insults, with distresses, with persecutions, with difficulties, for Christ's sake; for when I am weak, then I am strong" (2 Corinthians 12:9-10).

The Lord wants to break us for our own good, so that we can love Him with a purer, stronger love. I'm so thankful that I love Him a million times more than I did last year, and I pray my devotion to Him continues to swell. "Hear, O Israel! The LORD is our God, the LORD is one! And you shall love the LORD your God with all your heart, and with all your soul, and with all your might. And these words, which I am commanding you today, shall be on your heart" (Deuteronomy 6:4-6). *I love You, Father. Thank you for setting me free. Your love makes me see who I really am, a sinner who was saved by grace and is now a daughter of the mighty King, whom I will love to the bitter end. But thank you, too, for teaching me that I am only responsible for myself in the end.*

THANKSGIVING 2005

NOVEMBER 26, 2005–THANKSGIVING
61 DAYS OUT OF SURGERY!

"I will give thanks to Thee, for I am fearfully and wonderfully made; Wonderful are Thy works, And my soul knows it very well."

—Psalm 139:14

The LORD has given all of us more than we could ever deserve. He didn't have to create us; He doesn't need any of us, yet He longs for a relationship with us, for us to just stop and listen to Him. I can sense in my spirit that I need to take time away from home and stand still before my God. A lot of irons are in the fire right now. Of course, He already knew that when this whole process started, and He's just waiting for me to acknowledge that I can't make one move (at least not a wise one) without His guidance. I can't trust myself alone.

For me, I have a hard time sometimes distinguishing between His voice and my own. I don't want to put God in a box, yet I also don't want to say that my discernment is telling me something when in all actuality that's the *last* thing the Lord wants for me. At the same time, who am I to mess up God's plans? I'm reminded of Job 38 and 39, where God asked Job all these rhetorical questions, displaying His great power and glory and Job's frailty and total dependence on His heavenly Father. *Oh, Lord, I want to feel oh so small every single moment of my life, because I know that less of me means more of You.* As long as I'm honestly seeking His will, He's faithful and just to perform it. I just have to get out of the way and let Him move.

I want to fall facedown before my Holy God. I want to be where *He* wants me to be, but I'm finding that my pride is trying to sneak back up on me. It's the sin that so easily entangles me in its deceitful web if I'm not careful. I want to walk blamelessly before my Father, but I know that I mess up so many times every single day. I'm so glad God continues to take me back, dust me off, and show me yet again how much He *loves* me, how much He wants to use me.

I thought I'd list some of the things I'm thankful for. I won't, nor could I, compile a list that would truly display how gracious my Lord has been to me, but here's a start:

Jesus Christ-my Savior, Healer, First Love, and Coming King :

Lord, You are everything to me, and nothing I could ever say would convey my devotion to You. You are the reason I live, the song that I sing, and the force that drives me to righteousness. Lord, I am striving to become more like You every day. I know I fail, but I am so thankful for Your love, Your tenderness and, most of all, for the fact that You do give and take away (Job 1:21). I love You, I love Your church, and I love the freedom I find in Your arms. I'm ready to fly, Jesus; take me wherever You need me.

My Family-my mom, my dad, Holly, and everyone else:

They have had to live with me for almost twenty years now, and I know the road hasn't been easy in *numerous* ways. But I'm thankful that they've stuck by me, especially Mom and Dad. I *know* that I have no idea just how *much* you all have gone through; it couldn't have been easy watching your little girl struggle for every breath, wondering what the future held. The Lord *delivered* us, though, and I *know* He has a plan for each and every one of us. We didn't walk through that valley just for the sake of doing it, and, as we've already seen, for some reason we've been blessed with the vast responsibility and privilege of being witnesses to a miracle. I know I remind them all often that I *am* almost twenty years old and that living at home isn't always easy. But that doesn't mean I don't love and cherish each of them. I just have a wild heart, that's all; I'm independent, driven, passionate and, yes, I know, at times those strong characteristics get the best of me. I *do* know this, though: I'm a dreamer, and I'm ready for Him to take us higher. All praise and honor be to *His* name as we journey on together.

My Friends-To know them is my greatest earthly joy:

I don't even know where to begin. I know I tell them all the time how mesmerized I am by the fact that the good Lord gave me each and every one of them. But hearing it one more time won't hurt. Saying, "I love you," doesn't even begin to express the sheer delight I get from just hearing their voices on the phone, let alone when we get to sit down and be dead honest with each other in person. They say that a person is lucky if she goes through life with one best friend. If that's the case, I think I've broken the bank with all of my friends.

Sometimes at night I lie in bed and smile (and cry) thinking about everything we've gone through together. The journey started over a year ago, and it hasn't seemed to slow down since. The road has been full of uncertainty, but we held on to each other and, most importantly, we put all our trust in Him. Days grew colder, then warmer, then cooler once more. Even without answers, we pressed on. I say we because it was us, not just me. It seemed like every time I did not think for the life of me that I could go any further, one of my friends would call or come over. I am well aware that the prayers of my friends each and every moment of every day have sustained me. In March, we gathered together on that cold Sunday evening and planned my funeral. The next time we're all together, we can stand together in awe of our Savior's power. We may cry, but the reason will be entirely different than it very well could have been.

Cedarville University-Where I learned how to fly :

On that beautiful campus I lost everything I held so dear. But in return I gained so much more than I could have ever dreamed. Security in mere humans and even good health pales in comparison to the richness that comes from knowing Jesus Christ, my Lord. Whether or not I ever come back as a student or not, it doesn't matter. The impression has already been made on my heart, and I will never forget the change He began in me while I was there. Because I knew Cedarville, I have been changed for good. No matter where life takes me, I will never forget what we witnessed together, how blessed I am to know such amazing brothers and sisters in Christ. I'd do it all over again, as long as I could go through it with all of them. "But whatever things were gain to me, those things I have counted as loss for the sake of Christ. More than that, I count all things to be loss in view of the surpassing value of knowing Christ Jesus my Lord, for whom I have suffered the loss of all things, and count them but rubbish in order that I may gain Christ, and may be found in Him, not having a righteousness of my own derived from the Law, but that which is through faith in Christ, the righteousness which comes from God on the basis of faith, that I may know Him, and the power of His resurrection and the fellowship of His sufferings, being conformed to His death; in order that I may attain to the resurrection from the dead. Not that I have already obtained it or have already become perfect, but I press on so that I may lay hold of that for which also I was laid hold of by Christ Jesus. Brethren, I do not regard myself as having laid hold of it yet; but one thing I do: forgetting what lies behind and reaching forward to what lies ahead, I press on toward the goal for the prize of the upward call of God in Christ Jesus" (Philippians 3:7-14).

May we all press on to the higher calling that He has for each and every one of us, not wishing we were someone else but striving to be what He would have us to be, giving thanks in all things. As we enter the Christmas season, may we keep our eyes fixed on the heavens, with the Holy Spirit as our compass. He is all we need.

Reflections

Rachel:

I did not have the opportunity to know Amber real well before her surgery. I did not have the opportunity to sit at her bedside with her and have deep life conversations. I did not have the opportunity to take part in planning her funeral. I did not have the opportunity to get the call from her just minutes before being wheeled in for her incredible surgery. Despite all of this, I was granted many opportunities before I even knew Amber.

I have had the opportunity to be ministered to by Amber when she came, oxygen tank and all, to one of the summer *Teens for Christ* meetings, "The Slice." As we sang praises to our King, I remember her praising God through each coughing spell that tried to overcome her. Despite any and all obstacles, Amber persevered, knowing that the God she served was bigger than anything that might come her way. I did not do much singing that night. I remember praying for Amber's strength and for her weakness. That night I made a conscious decision to be in continual prayer for Amber, whom I knew so little about.

I had the opportunity to be ministered to by Amber one Saturday night in the fall of 2005. Amber was brought to Saturday Night Prayer by a mutual friend just as we were hearing the stories of praises and concerns of the *Teens for Christ* ministry. This frail teenage woman then began to speak, and she ministered and encouraged me more than I can put into words. She was encouraging us to be proactive. By using her testimony to bring to life the fact that we are not guaranteed anything in life, including time, she encouraged each of us to utilize the time that God has so graciously given us so that we can do the most for Him during our lifetime.

I had the opportunity to attend the TFC Kick-off on September 24, 2005, where Buck Sutton announced to all in attendance that Amber had gotten a call from Columbus and that this one was *the* one! I was so excited to hear this wonderful news. Finally, this girl whom I had never even talked to one-on-one, for whom I had been praying for months, and for whom I had been requesting others to pray was finally going to receive her life-saving and life-changing transplant. As I traveled an hour and a half back to be with my family at my cousin's wedding reception, nearly all of that time was spent in prayer for Amber, the doctors, and her loved ones. Upon arrival at the reception, I excitedly told my aunt and mom of the miracle: "Amber got her lungs!" By all of my excitement one would have thought that Amber and I had been friends for years.

After Amber's remarkable recovery from her surgery, I began to see her more and more at *Teens for Christ* meetings, Saturday Night Prayer, various Bible studies, and such. I was able to learn so much from her simply by listening to her speak in group discussions. After one of these gatherings, we spoke for the first time one-on-one and our friendship began to bud. Then in mid-January at Saturday Night Prayer, Amber approached me and we discussed and then prayed about our personal spiritual struggles, questions, and stances. We quickly discovered that we were both in, what we like to call the same "spiritual boat": a similarity that brought us even closer to each other. We determined that we had to spend more time with each other to talk and simply have fun. Two weeks later we saw each other for seven days straight. During that week-long period we were able to share even more about our lives and simply have a wonderful time together. We had the opportunity to laugh together, learn together, cry together, pray together, and grow closer. Despite the fact that we had only actually known each other for a couple of short months, it was if we had been friends for years.

Over the past few months I am not even able to recall all of the laughs shared, lessons learned, tears shed, prayers said, or meaningful discussions had with Amber. We had been brought together and God granted us amazing opportunities to grow closer to each other and closer to Him through each other.

I am thankful for many things in my life, one of which is that Amber Nicole Metz never allowed cystic fibrosis to overcome her, physically or spiritually. Because of this and God's gift of life and a successful transplant, I have had many amazing opportunities to learn and grow from Amber. Sometimes God gives us more than we alone can handle, but He never gives us more than we can handle with Him. I am grateful that Amber knows this and continues to hold on to it; for without that, Amber and I would not have had the opportunities that we have had.

I may not have had many of the opportunities to share in Amber's life leading up to her surgery that some had, but I have been given many opportunities since then and I am forever changed because of those God-given opportunities. Thank you, Amber. Thank you, God!

December 12, 2005–So Much More
78 days since surgery!

I have *so* many dreams. The last couple of weeks it has been a journey trying to figure out exactly where I fit in the grand scheme of things. I know I'm not called to work in every facet of ministry nor should I even attempt to stick my foot into some areas at all. My heart's desire for His church and His people is to see them come to know Him and experience true freedom in His name; at the same time, I'm struggling to hone in on what that means now.

As Christmas Day approaches, I know my writing to so many of my friends is almost over. That fact is a bittersweet one from me. I have felt so close to them over the past nine months and to move on and see what He has next is almost scary. I'll admit it: I'm quite comfortable doing this facet of ministry. In fact, I *love* to sit down, collect my thoughts, and share them with all of my email friends. I know He's used me-praise God-to enrich some people's spiritual walks. Each one means more to me than they will ever realize this side of eternity. Being able to be open and real with so many people has been a sobering yet freeing experience. My ghosts are out of my closet, I've learned to love and let go, and I'm continuing to see that it is only through Jesus Christ that I feel complete. I know I'm not extremely close to many of my email friends, but just the fact that they've opened up their inbox and read these messages from me means so much.

I pray that what I have said, or will say, is tested against Scripture (1 John 4:1-8). God is love, and I pray that all have felt His love and conviction in their lives. I know I have. It's not about what we have done or are going to do for Him in the future; it's about being faithful now.

Galatians 5:22-26:

"But the fruit of the Spirit is love, joy, peace, patience, kindness, goodness, faithfulness, gentleness, self-control; against such things there is no law. Now those who belong to Christ Jesus have crucified the flesh with its passions and desires. If we live by the Spirit, let us also walk by the Spirit. Let us not become boastful, challenging one another, envying one another."

As I walk on into the unknown, I do trust Him, but I'm constantly saying the verse, "Lord, I do believe; but help my unbelief" to myself (Mark 9:24). I am seeing that the healthier I get, the more my pride is becoming an issue with us. In Jesus name, I ask that it leave. I know that it will be my downfall if I allow Satan to get a foothold into my life. I'm not using satanic attacks as an excuse, but I must remember that Satan is like a lion, seeking whom he can destroy.

I Peter 5:8-11 reminds us:

"Be of sober spirit, be on alert. Your adversary, the devil, prowls around like a roaring lion, seeking someone to devour. But resist him, firm in your faith, knowing the same experiences of suffering are being accomplished by your brethren who are in the world. And after you have suffered for a little while, the God of all grace, who called you to His eternal glory in Christ, will Himself perfect, confirm, strengthen, and establish you. To Him be dominion forever and ever. Amen."

Alone, I cannot resist Satan. He knows which tactics work on me; he's the second most powerful presence in this world. But I also remember that Jesus Christ holds the keys to death and hell (Revelation 1:18). He's the Alpha and Omega, who is and who was and who is to come (Revelation 1:8). In the end, none of us will be able to resist or deny God's holiness. "Holy, Holy, Holy is the LORD of Hosts" (Isaiah 6:3) One day every knee will bow, and every tongue will confess that Jesus Christ is Lord of all (Romans 14:11). I want to bow now, to fall facedown before Him daily, and to show Him that I love Him through my obedience to His infallible Word.

Romans 15:17-18: "Therefore in Christ Jesus I have found reason for boasting in things pertaining to God. For I will not presume to speak of anything except what Christ has accomplished through me, resulting in the obedience of Gentiles by word and deed." I'm living in the mystery. I do make decisions, but God's sovereignty ultimately reigns, according to Psalm 103:15-22.

I want my life to be a reflection of His glory, to leave a legacy of love. It is my desire to leave the legacy of a woman who fears the Lord, speaks truth in love, and spreads her wings and does great things for the kingdom. 'Great things' doesn't necessarily mean seeing millions come to know the Lord through my testimony or seeing my book on the shelves of stores across the nation. I just want to be faithful where I am now; to love until I have nothing left to give; to disciple my younger sister, to love my parents with a pure, respectful love, to speak truth to my friends, even if that should mean that the friendships are broken because of it. I don't want to allow my fear of the unknown to steal my joy; my pride must be kept under control, and I must continue to realize who I am in Christ, not being ashamed of the personality that He gave me.

Life is a balance, I've realized. You win some and you lose some, but the important thing is you get back up and dust yourself off, pushing yourself forward for the kingdom, learning from your mistakes instead of dwelling on how much of a failure you are, and having a teachable spirit when older, wiser Christians give you that much-needed advice that you'd rather just ignore.

I will never meet my full potential for Christ unless I am willing to serve God and my fellow man. I know that sometimes serving God feels like it's taking every morsel of strength I have within me. But just in time, He always comes through. I want to be completely surrendered to His plans for my life and walking in the Light as He is in the Light (1 John 1:7). In fact, Jesus said that we'd see greater things in our time than He himself ever saw while He was on earth. The same Spirit that raised Jesus Christ from the dead lives within us, if we know Him.

God opposes the proud but gives grace to the humble (James 4:6), and He's more than willing to use a contrite spirit. On the days I am all wrapped up in myself, my spirit is not at ease, because I know that He can't use me the way I am; my pride is keeping me from the joy of the Lord. Surrender is probably the hardest thing to do, but I'm finding that as I daily surrender everything over to Him, He's ready to meet me with open arms. He already knows what I'm thinking, so nothing is a surprise to Him.

We can change the world; I'm convinced of that. Every fiber within me says it's possible. The disciples were accused of turning the world upside down, and they were made out of the same kind of DNA as us. I sometimes think that somehow people who walked with Jesus were super humans, but they were not. I want to expect and experience the supernatural. There is so much more to discover in Jesus' name, and I'm ready to go and climb the mountains, feel His presence in the small things, hear the rustle of the trees, love him with all I have and see Him blow my mind. How about you?

DECEMBER 22, 2005–THE ULTIMATE PARADOX 88 DAYS SINCE SURGERY!

Time seems to be passing so quickly anymore. I'm having a hard time keeping up. I look at the calendar and I'm amazed at the fact that it's almost Christmas. I wasn't sure I'd ever live to see Thanksgiving, let alone be alive and well at the end of December.

Life's a journey—a delicate balance that requires daily submission to His Word and His ways. The moment I think I have it all figured out, I truly have no idea. The more I try to figure out how to keep the pendulum from swinging too far to one side or the other, the more frustrated and confused I become. Jesus is not the author of confusion (1 Cor. 14:33) though, and I must stand on His promises, knowing that part of faith is being ok with living in the mystery. I'm not supposed to figure it all out. If I were, what would be the point of praying to my heavenly Father for guidance, for wisdom, and for strength? If I knew what I was doing I'd be a pretty self-sufficient person. The last time I checked, the Word firmly teaches that I am supposed to find my completion in Christ and Christ alone instead of in my mere knowledge (Col. 2:8-14).

I know that we're called to walk in the Light as He is in the Light (1 John 1:7), and boldly speaking truth to the masses in Jesus' name (Ephesians 4:14-32). How does one do this in today's society without coming across as militant? I want to stand firmly on truth, boldly proclaiming Christ crucified (1 Cor. 1:23), yet I want to love the way Jesus has commanded me to (Deut. 6:4-9. At times, I don't really know what I'm supposed to say or how I'm supposed to say it.

It's so much easier to follow a religion than it is to follow Jesus. With Jesus, I don't know what will happen, and I find myself swept up in something so much bigger than I could ever imagine, while with mere religion, people follow a set of guidelines already laid out for them without much thought as to why they serve God or whom they are called to love.

I think Jesus had such a different idea of what the church should be and what we should stand for. I think if we'd get out of our comfort zones more often, allowing God to show Himself, we'd be better off. If the ones who supposedly know Jesus don't speak the truth in love, who will? Something inside of me tells me there's more if I'd only open up my eyes.

If people become "projects" instead of precious children created in God's image, we sometimes focus more on getting people saved instead of loving them and praying that our own lives would be a reflection of His glory. It is better to ask in Jesus' name for the Holy Spirit to convict them of their sins, much the same way as we were convicted of our own sins. After all, it is not we who save souls but the power of the Holy Spirit coming upon an individual in a miraculous way. At the same time, sin is sin and we should call it what it is. Without the power of the Spirit inside, though, people can be blinded to the fact that unless they come to Christ, they will be apart from Him forever.

I've been thinking a lot recently about the word "Christian." What does that mean? Anyone can say he's a "Christian." If I go to some other country and state that I am a Christian, they might think I am the same as some Hollywood star. To be a Christian is simply to be an American, at least to many in the world. Why is this so? Why aren't we truly living out the Great Commission (Matthew 28:18-20) and providing an adequate answer for the hope within us (1 Peter 3:15)? I believe with all my heart that if I were to be a true disciple of Jesus there'd be no question as to why Jesus is the Hope of the world. Other religions may offer hope, but the only eternal hope is through Jesus Christ, our Lord (Ephesians 1:9-21). If all it means to be a Christian is to be a part of some political or militant agenda, or means following a set of doctrinal statements while ignoring the lost and dying world, then I don't even want to be called a Christian. What's the point? How is that mindset bringing people to Jesus?

I think I should be asking myself, "What would Jesus do?" more often. Was He not the man who had dinner with swindlers and prostitutes and drove the Pharisees (the religious ones of the time) mad? People try to tame Jesus, to make Him out to be some cookie-cutter figure to pattern our lives after. I think in doing that, we lose so much of who He was and what He wants to do in our lives through the power of the Spirit.

I see nowhere in the Gospels where Jesus played it safe and stayed away from sinners. At the same time, His testimony was never compromised. Jesus said we'd see even greater things done in His name than even He did during His time on earth and that the same power that raised Jesus from the dead lives within me.

I don't understand why this Man, who could have been born anywhere in the world, chose to be born in a barn. All I know is He humbled Himself and became a servant to all (Phil. 2:8). As Paul said, it has been granted to me for Christ's sake not only to believe in Him but also to suffer for His sake (Phil. 1:29). I can sit around and discuss the five percent of the Bible that divides so many churches today or I can start doing the ninety-five percent that is as clear as day. I love sitting around and having deep theological discussions, but why can't we just obey Him and love Him the way we should in the smallest things? Why can't we live out the holistic gospel with such a passion and fervency that we feel the mountains tremble? Was Pentecost just a one-time deal and now we're just trying to get by until Jesus comes back? Let it not be so.

Sitting in a theater watching *Narnia*, I was overwhelmed with emotion. I think we are living out that battle scene every single day of our lives, whether we realize it or not. That means we must put on the whole armor of God (Eph. 6:10-18) in order to be able to walk fully in the Spirit. The closer we get to the Father, the more Satan will attack you. We don't want to be blindsided. "With all prayer and petition pray at all times in the Spirit, and with this in view, be on the alert with all perseverance and petition for all the saints, and pray on my behalf, that utterance may be given to me in the opening of my mouth, to make known with boldness the mystery of the gospel" (Ephesians 6:18-19). Paul, one of the greatest theologians ever, was aware of the mystery.

Once the Spirit of God has unveiled our eyes, we no longer have any excuses. The more truth we expose ourselves to, the more accountable we are to that truth. I've seen that many times in my own life. I want people to see that I love Jesus, and that I desperately need His guidance in my life. I don't understand how

I've been saved, am being saved, and one day will stand before the Lord with a glorified body, but I know it's true. I know that situations in my life have shaped who I am and that although I fall numerous times a day, He's ready to pick me back up, dust me off, and lead me on.

Jesus is a paradox; there's no getting around that. I am never going to figure Him out this side of heaven. Yet with the help of the Holy Spirit, I can learn truth and walk in His ways. One day what I see in part I will fully know (1 Cor. 13:12), and Satan will be vanquished and I will reign with Jesus forever. Until then I struggle with the tension called life, begging the Father to show Himself to me, and praying that He and those around me will find me faithful.

CHRISTMAS DAY 2005

DECEMBER 25, 2005–MERRY CHRISTMAS DAY #91 OUT OF SURGERY!

I honestly did not know if this day would come for me, but here we are–Christmas Day 2005. Another year is coming to a close, and I am reminded once more that there has *always* been so much more going on than what it seems at first.

This part of my journey has come to an end; I'm ready to venture off into the unknown, knowing that God is right by my side, guiding me every step of the way. It is impossible to express everything that has gone through my mind. I'm just giving Him the keys and allowing Him to work through me. I've learned by now that any time *I* try to say anything without consulting the Lord first, I fall flat on my face afterwards. I know full well that I need His grace, hope, and love to see me through (1 Corinthians 13:13).

So many have walked this journey with me through the past nine months. I'm grateful to the ones who have pushed me for righteousness' sake, calling me out and critiquing me because they love me. God didn't *have* to use me, but I am *so* very glad He chose me to walk this road, to learn to die to myself, to learn of His immeasurable grace (1 Cor. 15:1-21). I have no idea what the future holds for me, but judging by the path He's had me tread thus far, I will not be the *least* surprised if I end up somewhere *completely* different than I expected.

Three months ago my life changed, and it surely hasn't slowed down since. September 25, 2005, is a day that will live in infamy in the lives of my family and friends. Over the course of a little over a year, Jesus changed me forever. My mindset, my heart, and my will were made *free*, and I can truly attest to the statement that "If therefore the Son shall make you free, you *shall be* free indeed" (John 8:36). Over, 2000 years ago, a son was born in a stable outside of Bethlehem to a teenage mother, and the world has never been the same since (Luke 2:7). I don't know much, but I know that Jesus Christ came to seek and save the lost and that He is Wonderful Counselor, Mighty God, Eternal Father, Prince of Peace (Isaiah 9:6); He's the Lamb of God who came to take away the sins of the world (John 1:29). He's also the Alpha and the Omega; there *truly* is no shadow of turning with Him. I walked through the valley of the shadow of death, yet He *was* with me and He certainly did see me through (Psalm 23:4). *All* my praise goes to my beautiful Savior on this day and *every* day of the rest of my life.

Not only was there the sacrifice my Jesus paid on the cross of Calvary for the redemption of my soul but also there was a family who donated their precious son or daughter's organs so that others might experience the gift of life through their tragic loss. I will **never** fully understand what they have gone through in the past months. As I have continually improved, they are faced with the harsh reality that their loved one is no longer with them. I'm sure that especially today, on Christmas, emotions are raw and their pain severe. I admit that I probably do not take as much time as I should to ponder not only Jesus paying my ransom but the *precious* **voluntary** gift I was given here on earth three months ago.

Words will *never* be able to express to my donor family my gratitude. I pray that I will honor Jesus and their son or daughter as I daily fall on my knees, asking Him to show me where to walk, what to say, and how to serve Him and my fellow man. Jesus gave me eternal life, yes, but a family's selfless act gave me a second chance to *live* for Him.

At times, I would pay to go back to how I felt right before my surgery, if only just for a few minutes. To feel that desperation for my Lord, that *constant* crying out of His name, *that* is my only wish for this Christmas season. I don't even want to live if I'm not **completely** surrendered to my Sweet Jesus.

As I celebrate Christmas, I want to remember that, although it sounds like a cliché, Jesus *is* the reason for the season. If there were *any* other way to the Father but through Jesus Christ (John 14:6), there would have been **no** reason for Him to come, to walk on this earth as a man, humbling Himself for you and for me (Philippians 2:5-11). Through *Him* I find new life, not through *anything* else, even two new lungs. I want my life to be a reflection of His glory and for the statement, "Jesus breathes in, I breathe out." to be true in my life.

God owns the cattle on a thousand hills (Psalm 50:10), but we were the only creatures He created in *His* image (Gen. 1:26). You and I display to the world the image of God—or we are *supposed* to do so. How others who don't know Him perceive our Savior comes from how well *we* reflect His attributes. After all, we *are* His hands and feet.

The more I learn about Christ, the more I long to know Him better, I know that I have *so* many misconceptions about Him and the ways He wants to work through and among us. My heartfelt prayer is that I will be discerning yet *open* to see Him move, to be able to feel the mountains tremble and people young and old, come to Jesus. I want to walk where angels fear to tread, to **go** where He's sent me (Matthew 28:18-20), to passionately stand on truth (John 8:31-32), and to know beyond a shadow of a doubt that He has sent the Holy Spirit to guide me, to mold me, and to draw me closer to Him (John 14:16, 26).

I take courage in 1 Corinthians 13:12, "For now we see in a mirror dimly, but then face to face; now I know in part, but then I shall know fully just as I also have been fully known." I can't figure it all out here on earth, but I'm thankful I *can* stand on His Word and the truths that He has revealed to me thus far. As a good friend reminded me, I am not any of my favorite authors, nor am I supposed to be. I'm just *Amber*, and it's my duty to try to fulfill the calling He has placed on *my* life. I don't care if people know my name; I just want them to see Jesus, the One who died for me and bought me back my freedom (Isaiah 61:1).

Since when are we called to be safe Christians, anyway? I'd rather laugh in the face of danger and march straight into the battlefield for countless souls' hearts and minds. It is only in the trenches that we see Jesus working; He *never* worked from the sidelines, and I don't think we are called to do so, either.

I've lost much here on earth to gain the surpassing knowledge of knowing Jesus Christ (Phil. 3:8-14), and I count my suffering as *joy*. I'm thankful that "God has chosen the foolish things of the world [me] to shame the wise, and God has chosen the weak things of the world to shame the things which are strong" (1 Cor. 1:27). Lord knows I screw up countless times a day, but He continues to pick me back up, dust me off, and lead me Home (Micah 7:7-8).

There really isn't anything left to say. For it is here that I'm finally free, here that I see what I was created to do-worship Him with *every* breath-no matter what befalls me. I pray He has spoken to others through *anything* I have had to say and that it is always His words and not my own. I may not be very eloquent or a great theologian, but I love Jesus, and my desire is to know *Him* more, to live a life that lives and breathes to give Him joy. If we call out to Him, not for our own self-worth but for His will and delight, He will give you rest, of this I'm sure.

Well, I guess I'm supposed to end with some rousing speech of some sort or fiery words of conviction, but I think I'd rather just say that I sincerely love this privilege and responsibility that Christ has bestowed upon me. Saying thank you to friends and family for lifting me up in prayer all these months just doesn't cut it, but it seems the English language doesn't offer me many other words to choose. When we all get to see Jesus and each other one day in Heaven, I cannot wait to sit and talk with all of you, to hear what the Lord has done in your lives; after all, it's not about me at all. It is about Jesus and community, about living and dying for our Savior and becoming free in Him. Wherever I go, wherever He allows me to speak, whatever I do, I pray with fervency that I never lose sight of that simple truth.

I thought I knew love before I started on this journey, but I had *no* idea about the unfathomable love of Christ. I can't describe how deep or wide that love is exactly, but I know that it's real, it's available, and is *so* much better than anything here on earth. Human love will fail, people are bound to let us down, but I do know one thing: The world has tried to stamp out His name, turn Christmas into a time to boost the economy, and replace our sacred traditions with Frosty the Snowman and Rudolph, but Jesus Christ is the same yesterday, today, and forever (Hebrews 13:8). Amen.

I leave you with this prayer:

"Therefore, since we receive a kingdom which cannot be shaken, let us show gratitude, by which we may offer to God as an acceptable service with reverence and awe; for our God is a consuming fire."

—Hebrews 12:28-30

Father,

Consume us. Break us. Mold us. Use us. Show us. We need more of You..Amen.

All for my Precious Savior,
Amber Nicole Metz

SEPTEMBER 25, 2007

Amber's two-year anniversary

- FEV1 is up to 100%, as of early October 2007
- Feeding tube was removed in early 2006, after being dependent on it for extra nutrition for over two years
- In the first two years, Amber has shown no signs of rejection and continues to amaze her physicians.
- Amber has spent the past two years feverishly working on, editing, and formatting *Breathtaking* from more than 750 pages of emails written in a ten-month period.
- *Breathtaking* is a testament to God's grace, Amber's love offering to her Savior, Healer, and Coming King. This book would not be possible without the gracious financial donations given in 2006 from churches and individuals who believed the Lord could use Amber's story to change lives and draw hearts closer to Himself.
- For more information on *Breathtaking Ministries,* please visit www.ambermetz.com
- For information on cystic fibrosis, please visit: www.cff.org.
- For information on how to become an organ donor, please visit www.donatelife.org.

Epilogue

"The heartbeat of our faith is not achieving great things with God, nor is it doing great things with God. Our deepest longing is simply to be with God, to know Him as Friend and Father, to trust Him as Savior, and thus, to obey Him as Lord."

—Pete Greig, *The Vision & The Vow*[15]

SEPTEMBER 4, 2006–SEND ME

Who am I? No, truly, who is Amber Nicole Metz? On this fourth day of September 2006, just days away from the one-year anniversary since my double lung transplant, who am I and where am I going? Where have I been? Does it really matter?

I will wait on You, Lord.
I will wait on You.
Please...
Make me the Breath of God..

So to answer my own question: I'm not sure who I am or where I'm going, but I know that the Lord does, and that's all that really matters to me. I know that even in the past weeks I've changed, and I want to continue to grow, to struggle, to learn. I never want to lose sight of where He has taken me, of the divine privilege and responsibility I feel I have been given. I will wait, for I know that the plans He has for me are not to harm me but to give me a hope and a future (Jeremiah 29:11). For me, that simply means that He will go before me and prepare the way. No, the way may not be what I had planned (it never is), but I love living in the mystery. I don't want all the answers; I want to be satisfied with just knowing Him and trusting in His sovereignty. I know He has called me, and what will happen was set in stone before the foundation of time. I know I'm only a vapor here for a short while (James 4:14), but there is so much one can accomplish in His name, of this I'm sure.

I'm thankful that He never gives us more than we can handle at the time, that He makes us wait for our own good, not to punish us but to mold us into the men and women He wants us to be in His perfect timing. I'm thankful that the Son has set me free, and I am free indeed (John 8:36). I'm thankful that the past twelve months have been extremely difficult in many ways, much more challenging than lying in bed and frequently divulging all my thoughts to hundreds of people.

I've learned-and still am learning-how to live alone, how to effectively communicate truth to individual people, how truth and grace work together, how to worship Him in spirit and in truth, how to not forsake my passion and boldness for a tamer personality while at the same time not using it as an excuse for not yielding to the Holy Spirit. Most of all He has taught me how to let the people and the things I love the most go and realize that life does indeed change and as Dietrich Bonhoeffer would say, "When Christ calls a man, He bidst him come and die."[16]

I've been called to not only go but to bring unity to the body of Christ as a whole, to look at things objectively and pray and search for truth, to allow myself to be put in situations where I will inevitably be stretched beyond my comfort zone. I will go and I will follow, not because I don't have a choice, because I very much do as many people show every single day, but because I have yielded the free will that Christ Himself gave me to Him and to Him alone. *Breathtaking* and Breathtaking Ministries are only in existence because of the mighty, awesome, power of my Lord Jesus Christ. I take no credit for how He has, and will continue, to use me. But at the same time, I take full responsibility for the mistakes I've made on the way and the ones I'm sure to make. I'm not perfect, but I'm willing to go, to pay any cost on this earth for the surpassing knowledge of knowing Jesus Christ as my Lord (Philippians 3:7-9).

> "Delight thyself also in the LORD; and he shall give thee the desires of thine heart."
>
> —Psalm 37:4 (KJV)

I'm trusting and believing in that statement, as I say:

Lord, my one and only desire is to know You more. Use me, break me, burn within me with a passion that burns for only You. Empty me and fill me with more of You. Give me a heart to love You well, to give my all for the One who set me free and, in the process, to do Your work for Your kingdom.

So many opportunities are before me, and as I press on, I hear my Savior calling…

…so I say, "Here am I. Send me!"

—Isaiah 6:8

All my love,
Amber Nicole Metz

References

1. By John Piper. © Desiring God. Website: www.desiringGod.org. Email: mail@desiringGod.org. Toll Free: 1.888.346.4700.
2. A term used for the amount of air one can blow out in a one-second period. This measurement is a very important factor when addressing one's respiratory health. Once your number gets below 40%, transplant becomes a very real possibility and an increasing necessity.
3. The FEC measurement measures *total* lung capacity. Results are out of 100.
4. As mentioned before, the FEV1 measurement measures how much air one can blow out in a one second time period. The FEV1 is the number that is looked at most often when treating patients with cystic fibrosis.
5. Pulmonary Function Test
6. Erwin McManus, *The Barbarian Way* (Nashville: Thomas Nelson, Inc. 2005), 68-69.
7. Toledo Children's Hospital and Columbus Children's Medical Center use different standards for their Pulmonary Function

Tests. The percentages given by Toledo are subsequently lower than the ones given by the team at Columbus Children's Medical Center by an average of 5-7%. (ex. a 28% FEV1 according to Toledo would be around a 23% FEV1 from Columbus.

8. Song "In Christ Alone" by the Newsboys from the album *Adoration* (2003).

9. The hymn "It Is Well with My Soul" was written by Horatio Spafford in 1873 in mid-Atlantic, according to his daughter, Bertha Spafford.

10. Words by Elgar and original music by *New Haven Symphony Orchestra* in 1905.

11. Dietrich Bonhoeffer, *The Cost of Discipleship,* (New York: Touchstone. 1995), 89.

12. Rob Bell, *Velvet Elvis* (Grand Rapids, MI: Zondervan Publishing House. 2005), 169.

13. I want to personally thank Mark Driscoll for expounding upon this idea of embracing the incarnation and exaltation of Jesus at the 2006 *Desiring God National Conference* held in Minneapolis, MN, September 29 – October 1, 2006. The conference was titled *The Supremacy of Christ in a Postmodern World,* where Mark's thoughts centered around the Supremacy of Christ and the Church in a postmodern world. You can go to www.desiringGod.org and listen to the entire panel of speakers for free.

14. Remember, Columbus Children's uses a different measurement than Toledo Children's as their standard. If I had been going up to Toledo Children's during this time, my FEV1 would have registered even *lower.*

15. Pete Greig, *The Vision & The Vow,* (Lake Mary, FL: Relevant Books. 2004),.26.

16. Dietrich Bonhoeffer, *The Cost of Discipleship,* (New York: Touchstone. 1995), 89.

Printed in the United States
207087BV00001B/49/A

9 781414 108971